# DECIDE!

## ACTIVATE YOUR INNER SUPERPOWER TO MAKE VERY COOL SH*T HAPPEN

## DREW ROZELL, PH.D.

*very cool life*

# CONTENTS

# PREFACE

How do you lose twenty pounds?

How do you write your first book?

How do you break out of prison?

How do you get your car's oil changed?

How do live sober?

How do you find a partner?

How do you learn to play a favorite song on guitar?

How do you have a fabulous time at the party you really didn't want to attend?

How do you create an endless supply of money?

How do you have a better relationship with your kids?

How do you get pizza with pepperoni and mushrooms delivered to your door?

The fundamental answer to all these questions is the same.

You decide.

This is the stealth, underlying force that frames the unfolding of every aspect of your life.

Everything else is composed of details. Sure, you've got to follow through. You've got to take some actions. You've got to show up to your own life. But deciding, that is the skeleton key that unlocks all the doors that currently separate you from your desires. The desires are there for the taking, no matter how simple or grand, but first you must decide to ask for what you want.

The good news is that all of this is no big deal. As a human, you are built to function as a deciding machine. You've decided your way through life since the time you arrived into this world. (Some would say you're only in this human experience because you decided to come and take the ride.)

Deciding is your superpower.

And yet, because you are already a master decider, just as you are a master at breathing, it's easy and natural to let this power recede into the background of your awareness. But just as deliberately focusing on your breathing leads you to remember the power within your breath, **the main purpose of this book is to remind you how consciously activating your superpower to decide is the simplest, most powerful key to deliberately creating the outcomes you most want in your life right now.**

# PART I
# DECIDE

# THE VIEW STORY PART 1: DECIDING

*As a new parent, I quickly discovered the best way to get my babies to nap was to load them in my truck and venture out on a destination-free tour of our local country roads. We live in dairy farm country, among the rolling hills along the border of upstate New York and Vermont.*

*In addition to using these drives to induce little people to sleep, I'd use these outings as personal explorations, getting myself familiar as to where the nearby roads less traveled led. What the area lacks in terms of entertainment options or restaurants is made up for by the natural beauty of the land. The fact that our home has quite a lovely view turned me into somewhat of a "view junkie" and so I'd make note of the views from the properties I'd drive past. What did each homeowner see from their living room?*

*Driving through the hills, breathtaking vistas opened up around most every bend in the road. But to my eyes, of all the views I'd seen in the area, one stood a head taller than the rest.*

*WHEN I FIRST MOVED TO my home fourteen years ago, I hiked to the top of my property and saw my neighbors in their driveway heading into their house. I had my dogs with me, so I just gave them a friendly wave with the intention to introduce myself another day.*

*I never saw them again.*

*This was their second home and for whatever reason, they just stopped visiting the property. Around the same time, I began exploring it on my daily walks with the dogs. The first time I walked through the towering spruce trees that seemed to stand guard like a pair of sentinels and into the open hay field that lay beyond, I felt my spirit connect to the land.*

*Most anyone who appreciates a vista would, of course, and the panorama before my eyes was simply spectacular.*

*Ridge after ridge of rolling hills — I counted eight when the contrasting light was the sharpest — all framed by some of the highest peaks of the Green Mountains of Vermont.*

*I owned the nearly ten acres below that borders this hilltop property, and while we enjoy a remarkable east to southwest view from my home, it was not THIS view. This one spanned 270 degrees from the northern peaks of upstate New York, to the entire eastern border of Vermont, and all the way around back to New York State in the southwest.*

*The longer I drank in the view, I noticed how I felt as though this property was mine. As odd as it sounds, I felt as though this view in particular had been created just for me.*

*But my deed said something else.*

*However, for the next decade, I treated the property much as if I owned it. When taking friends around on a tour of my neighboring acreage, the grand finale was taking them an extra hundred yards from my property border, past the now-vacant house, over to the secret field that I'd cleverly dubbed "The View."*

*"Wait till you see this ..." I'd say as we began our gentle trespass to my neighbors' forgotten, quiet land.*

*After a year or two, a For Sale sign sprouted out of the lawn. For a split second, I felt a rocket of desire launch from my heart — I could buy The View! However, in the next moment, I felt the air brakes kick in. I already had a mortgage, a business that delivered no steady paycheck, and my wife and I were planning on starting a family soon. As much as I would love to have The View as my own, I had little use for the home that came attached to the property and even less interest in maintaining twenty-three more acres. Indeed, a quick online search informed me that the asking price was more than three times what I paid for my house and land.*

*However, this didn't stop me from dreaming about The View.*

*Every now and again my wife and I would bat around ideas of how we could turn this into a retreat center for our businesses. Or perhaps we could fix it up for rent? But as time passed and the house began showing more signs of neglect, entertaining these thoughts felt more like far-reaching fantasies than inspired ideas to act upon.*

*I also tried to convince my visiting friends and relatives on buying the place and become my neighbor. I rationalized that at least then I would always have access to The View and it would keep some monied foreigner from downstate from snapping it up and plastering the trees with bright orange POSTED signs. But no one bit.*

*Eventually the For Sale sign got crushed by the maintenance man plowing the access road to the property. No one replaced it. In all my walks up there, I never encountered a realtor or anyone beyond a worker cutting the grass. Every few months I'd look up the property online to see if there was a sale pending, but it was always sitting there on a low-traffic, local realtor's homemade listing, seemingly forgotten and never updated.*

*After the economic crash in 2008, the asking price lowered to nearly half of what it was a few years earlier. Upon seeing this, the rockets of desire launched again, this time with a little more thrust behind them. But for all my scheming, planning, and dreaming of ways to acquire the property, there was no path that I could conjure, no plan I could come up with to solve my "problem" of acquiring The View. It felt as if I was just about to finish a jigsaw puzzle and I had three pieces left, though no matter how hard I pressed, none of the pieces fit cleanly.*

*Now at the same time all this was occurring, I made my living from writing books and coaching my clients on living life in harmony with the laws of the universe and the process of deliberate creation. Certainly I remain a student of this approach to life as well and so with some stellar coaching from a mentor, I made a conscious decision to stop treating my desire for this property as a problem to be solved. Instead of trying to figure out ways to make the property mine, I decided to regularly connect to the feeling that the property was already mine.*

*Every time I'd make the trek up the hill to visit The View, I'd make a point to let the feeling of appreciation flow through me. When I had guests, I'd show the property to them and allow a sense of pride to wash through me as they'd oooh and aaah over "my view."*

*As more years passed, through my neighbors and local realtors, I'd hear about the history of offers that were made on the property. There were a handful, at least, and eventually all of them fell through for one reason or another. While these failed deals quietly pleased me, they also allowed me the time and space to ease into a state of letting go.*

*Sooner or later, the property was going to sell.*

*Instead of wishing for sales to fall through or praying for bags of money to fall from the sky onto my couch, I found myself picturing that my new neighbor was someone cool — you can never have enough friends when you live in the country. I imagined that the new owners wouldn't mind me crossing their property to admire the view on my cross-country skis or to continue sharing the vista with friends when they'd visit.*

*Then one early summer day, we took a family walk, strolling over to our neighbors' homestead to let our kids raid their bountiful berry crop. Al, the patriarch, had grown up in the area and knows everything about everyone.*

*He broke the news right away.*

*"The property up top sold, you know?" Al said.*

# WHAT DOES IT MEAN TO DECIDE?

WHAT DOES it mean to decide?

Well, the word can be traced back to Latin *decaedere*, where *de* means "off" and *caedere* means "cut".

So a literal translation is to "cut off."

And in this context, when you are deciding, you are *cutting off other possibilities.*

Think about that.

Better yet, FEEL that.

Feel how your energy shifts when you deliberately focus your intention on ONE outcome — what you really desire — having pruned all other potential outcomes like dying branches from a tree.

When you De-cide you are informing the universe, "This is what's happening next. This is what I will have. Just because I want it. In fact, I can feel its presence now just by deciding to have it. Done and done."

When you declare your desires in this manner, there is only one possible outcome — manifestation. Again, mechanically speaking, this is a simple process.

However, when we factor in some of the baggage that comes along with the human experience, very often we approach our desires much more tentatively, like a circling dog trying to find the perfect place to lie down.

On an outcome that feels really important to us (or maybe just plain fun), instead of commanding the course of our reality, we often take a "wait and see" approach or we "hope things work out."

What this really means is that on the feeling, vibrational level (the only level that matters in terms of what we create) we often approach our desires with a sense of anxiety, doubt, fear, or a meek curiosity instead of a certainty that it is done. In our thoughts, we haven't pruned any of the branches of possibility as to what we expect to unfold.

In these cases, we haven't truly made a deliberate decision. Note the lyric in the fantastic Rush song "Freewill": "If you choose not to decide, you still have made a choice." In other words, when you don't consciously decide exactly what you will have, you're still choosing, but by default and without intention.

In these instances, it's like walking into a random restaurant, tossing the menu aside, and telling the waiter, "Bring me whatever." You can't be surprised if the meal you're served is not to your liking. You can do better than creating by default. Much better.

But to do so, it's helpful to briefly review why deciding is such a critical aspect of getting what you really want.

## WHY IS DECIDING IMPORTANT?

Well, because deciding lies at the root of how life works.

Consider this: Everything you have in your life right now and all your past experiences, you have because you *decided* to have it.

And when you pause and really take notice, you'll become aware that at least 99% of your desires are present in your life right now. So stop for a moment. Look up and look around. Notice all the things that you are surrounded by. Put your attention on how many of your desires you have manifested (from the wonderful to the mundane).

As I mentioned in the preface, you are already a master manifestor. You already know how all this works and certainly you've made millions of decisions so far.

In fact you're so good at all of this that you only tend to notice (and dwell) upon the tiny fraction of all of your desires that are not here, right now in this red-hot minute. And again, my job with this book is to remind you how to allow more of those things, just for the fun of it.


## THERE ARE MIRACLES ALL AROUND YOU

Right now as I write this, I look around my office and I am surrounded by past desires that have manifested into reality. For example, on my desk next to me I have a fancy Japanese thermos of good coffee from South America. And I like it very much.

Now until this moment, I've never really thought about *how* this coffee came into my experience (let alone how the thermos got here from half a planet away in Japan). I don't know who harvested the beans, who processed them, who packed them, who shipped them thousands of miles, or any of the people involved in delivering them to my door (except our UPS guy, Phil, who totally rocks).

When I stop and think about it, the whole process is sort of a miracle, isn't it? It's all beyond my ability to understand how all the moving parts come together to fulfill my desire. I just want what I want, I take the simple, easy, obvious action (I swipe my thumb on the Amazon app) and *voila!*. Delicious, hot coffee inspires me out of bed each day.

When I wake in the morning, I simply expect coffee to happen, I harbor no internal resistance to this desire, and so coffee happens.

When you wake, you're not worrying about whether you can have your coffee, or whether there will be water available to make that coffee, or electricity to heat that water. You're not contemplating whether your lungs will exchange O2 for CO2, whether your heart will pump your blood, or whether your legs will support your body as you rise.

These are all miracles that occur as pieces of the fulfillment of your desires.

You've just *decided* that it will all be there, you cut off all other possibilities from your thoughts, you expected it, and so it is.

This is how *everything* in your life works.

Your life becomes a collection of miracles when you allow yourself to see your world this way and bask in the true power your decisions hold.

Now, obviously you don't sit around consciously pondering every particular detail of your life. You didn't choose to come into this human experience to sweat the small stuff. But part of the deal from your deciding to come into this world was that as a human, you get to experience the delight of having personal desires and feeling the wonder of them as they come into manifestation. This is how and why the Universe continually expands (but this is a story for another day).

So you have it because you've decided to have it, for you, my friend, are a master manifestor and the director of your reality.

Deciding is the fundamental spark that sets all of your desires down the path of manifestation. This (and a healthy dose of ALIGNING and ALLOWING) is all you need.

You don't need to meditate twice a day to get what you want. You don't need to create lists of intentions to study each day. You don't need start small or settle in your desires and then work your way up to the "bigger" things.

The whole point of this book is to remind you that no matter your desires, in order to create something you'd like, you never need to do anything but to make a decision and then get out of the way by following what feels better in the present moment and allowing that decision.

## I'M PRETTY SURE I DECIDED (MANY TIMES), SO WHY DON'T I HAVE WHAT I WANT?

Deciding really is just as simple as ordering a cup of coffee, and yet as straightforward as the mechanics of deciding are, and even though you are a master of deciding in so many aspects of your life, there are places where you likely feel like you're banging your head against a wall with regards to creating your desires. And I'll wager that's part of why you're reading this, so let's talk about it now.

So let's review what the whole process of deciding looks like again.

STEP 1. You focus. "Yes, I want this thing ..." (Decide)

STEP 2. You expect it to show up. (Align)

STEP 3. It manifests in your life as a function of the clarity of your expectation in STEP 2 when you simply don't get in the way. (Allow)

NOW THIS EXPECTING PART, as simple as it sounds, is where things tend to go off the rails.

Let's return to my coffee example for a moment.

When I order my coffee, I click a button on my phone and in two days it's on the porch.

I just take the obvious action of placing the order, and then I forget about it and move on with my life.

I never give the process a second thought. I'm not even remotely curious as to *how* this process of my manifesting coffee works. I hold no resistance to the idea that my coffee will show up. I don't worry about it. I'm not tracking its delivery. I'm not continually monitoring my porch to see if it's arrived.

And because I hold no resistance to my desire for coffee, because I just expect it to be so, at some point I'll open the door to let the dog out, and the miracle of a little brown box will be waiting for me. Easy.

Now what would happen if decided I wanted some more coffee, I took the action of ordering it, and then my coffee did not manifest?

In fact, this just happened recently as someone stole my package as it hung from a plastic bag on my mailbox at the end of my driveway. I saw it hanging there all day, but waited until my kids' bus arrived to retrieve it, and by then it was gone.

So what did I do when my desire failed to manifest in my experience?

Did I throw a fit?

Did I spend any time worrying about what went wrong in the manifestation process?

Did I blame myself?

Did I strategize how to protect myself from this happening again in the future in some way?

No.

It's just coffee, right? And this was just an inexplicable hiccup within a system that has worked seamlessly many times before.

So what did I do instead?

*I noticed what felt better to do in that moment and did it.*

(Really, this all you ever need to do.)

In this instance, I ordered more coffee. I went on with my life and it arrived as planned two days later.

But here's the thing to remember about your desires — it's *all* coffee.

A favorite teacher of mine, Abraham-Hicks, has a quote that goes like this: "It's as easy to create a castle as it is a button. It's a matter of whether you're focused on a castle or a button." In other words, the scope of your desire is irrelevant. To the Universe, the castle and the button are the same size and delivered the same way — through your focus and expectation.

The hot lover in your bed? The big number in your bank account? The lean, strong body? The shiny vehicle or a lovely home with view? The crisp, crunchy apple?

They are all the same.

The ONLY thing that differs among our desires is the degree to which we offer resistance to allowing them into our lives. Truly deciding means that you've dropped all your resistance — your worries, your fears, your ego, your curiosity — and allow yourself to align with the having of your desire. This may take some work, of course (and we'll talk about that shortly), but when it's done, that's all that needs to be done.

And this is why the process of deciding is worthy of your attention.

Because if it's not showing up, it's simply because you have not yet decided that it's yours. If it's not showing up, this is your clear feedback that you haven't cut off all other possibilities with regards to your expectations of what you will have.

The beauty of this kind of feedback is its perfection, clarity, and simplicity. When you see that these are the rules under which your personal universe is operating, then in any given moment, you can intentionally correct course to align yourself with what you want.

But truly embracing the power of deciding requires you to make a leap of faith.

## THE LEAP: YOU ARE THE DIRECTOR OF YOUR REALITY

You are the director of your reality.

Everything you see around you, all the experiences you've ever had — the ones you love, and the ones you really dislike — you're the creator of all of it.

100%.

No exceptions.

In short, you create all the experiences that you like.

And you create all the experiences that you don't like.

You are the director of every experience you ever had, and every experience is serving you and moving you closer to your desires.

Realizing the awesome power of deciding requires you to make the leap of taking radical responsibility for all your creations. This means that when you see things in your life that please you, you allow yourself to say, "I created this because I decided it was so."

And of course, when you see things in your life that do not please you, you allow yourself to say, "I created this because I decided it was so."

See how this works?

Yes, it's very simple. In theory.

In practice, of course, when things do not seem to be going according to plan, it's often not a natural headspace to enter.

And certainly there are plenty of unwanted situations in all of our lives that we cannot make sense of, and that would appear preposterous to think we "decided." More on this in a minute.

But for now, if you really want to live into the deliberate practice of deciding and reap the rewards of doing so, the only way it really works is if you are willing to take The Leap and then see what happens.

The Leap I am talking about asks you to see your life through this lens:

*If it shows up in my life, wanted or unwanted, it's because I summoned it through my focus, either deliberately or by default.*

Because if you don't see yourself as the active driver of your reality, a possessor of freewill, but rather the leaf blowing in the wind of the Universe or as the passenger along for the ride, then any attempt to harness the power of deciding (and reading further) would likely prove to be an unwise use of your time.

Over the years of coaching people to implement these principles, when looking at my clients' results, I had to admit they were mixed, at best. The perplexing thing was that 20% of the people began experiencing "miracles" while the other 80% saw little change from this work.

What was even more frustrating for many of the 80% was that they resonated deeply with these ideas, felt them to be true at their core, and yet they felt their realities failed to meet their expectations. Unwanted patterns continued to play on a loop.

After studying people in both groups, a clear pattern emerged, and it was this: Those who were willing to start seeing themselves as the creator of all their experiences and made inward adjustments started seeing more of what they were wanting. These people discovered that at the root of every miracle, there lies a decision they made, found alignment with, and allowed into their lives.

As for those who mentally understood the concept but failed to integrate much of it into their lives due to habits of blame, victimhood, or playing the role of intellectual skeptic? Things remained pretty stagnant or got worse for these folks.

Because until you own it all, you cannot change much of anything.

There's the old saying that with great power comes great responsibility. The inverse is also true: Great power comes from taking great responsibility.

Now, to be clear, to take The Leap, you don't need to believe this 100% right this minute. You may still have some "whatabouts" in your head where you have an anecdotal story you believe to be an exception to the rule. That's normal.

You just need to be willing to consciously try this perspective on.

The Leap asks you to set aside debating unanswerable questions, looking for reasons this could not possibly be the way life works, and falling into the default habit of blame when you don't like your current reality. Just be willing for a while … and then see what happens.

So, going forward, I'm going to assume that you've taken The Leap with me. You're willing and open. Because that's what it takes to leverage the power of deciding.

## WHY WOULD I DECIDE TO CREATE THINGS I DON'T LIKE?

Okay, so now you've made The Leap and you're willing to entertain that you are the creator of all of your experiences and that each one of your creations moves you in the direction of what you really want.

Embracing pleasant outcomes is quite easy. Taking ownership of our unwanted creations is hard.

After all, the question bears answering:

Why would I decide to create things I don't like?

Well, here's why:

Because without the night, there'd be no such thing as day.

Without knowing the taste of bitter, sweetness would cease to exist.

Without illness, you'd have no sense of vitality.

Without the cold, starkness of winter — well, you get the idea.

Contrast — experiences that we don't especially like (or sometimes really abhor) — are an integral part of the human experience.

Contrast is not to be avoided.

Trying to protect yourself from creating things you don't like is not only futile, but draws more unwanted things into your experience (because focusing on what you DON'T WANT always has a boomerang effect).

Rather, the contrast of unwanted creations and experiences is ever-present, completely natural, and deeply purposeful.

Contrast works like tinder to spark your power to DECIDE what you will have in your life. The sole purpose of contrast is that it be leveraged.

Contrast serves as the GPS coordinates telling you where you are now in relation to where you really want to go next. In other words, it's only by knowing what you do NOT want, that you arrive at the context and clarity to then identify and decide what you DO want.

Consider that you learned to walk because at some point you saw all these other bigger people moving around you with more freedom and ease and you decided that crawling around on your knees felt restrictive.

A rude encounter with a stranger clarifies your desire for kinder interactions.

An aching back focuses your desire to move freely and without pain again.

Looking at your bank account and feeling like there's not enough money sparks your desire to experience more.

The contrast of unwanted experiences provides the opportunity to shape your life in alignment with what you're really wanting.

That said, it's important to note that this isn't about putting lipstick on a pig or forcing a smile through a locked jaw in the face of things that suck.

Rather the point here is to remind you that this is how the Universe is organized. This is just the deal. Because when you know the rules of the game, and you choose to respect them, you have the opportunity to leverage the hell out of them.

And to leverage the contrast of life, you must DECIDE.

Specifically, in the face of unwanted feelings like pain, worry, stress, sadness, fear, or disease, you are never more clear in what you DON'T WANT.

Here's where the work comes in. In these moments, a willingness to show up with awareness, openness, and discipline allows you the opportunity to create what many people refer to as "miracles." (After a while of living and creating this way, having your desires show up in pleasing, unexpected ways will become the new normal.)

Instead of unconsciously dwelling in the headspace of how awful your unwanted experiences are (by far the most common default response to contrast), you'd be wise to step into your power as the deliberate creator of your experiences, to activate your inner superpower, and to DECIDE.

In the midst of contrast, the simplest way to do this is to ask yourself one simple question:

*"What is it that I DECIDE to have from here?"*

Going back to the previous unwanted examples, some new decisions going forward might look something like this:

*Everyone I meet is helping me get what I want.*

*I am ready to move my body with ease again.*

*I always have all the money I need to do as I want.*

Pretty simple stuff, right? Nothing too complicated. So, hopefully, now the critical role of contrast in the process of deciding and creation makes sense.

Again, the whole point of this book is to remind you that DECIDING is the most direct route to consistently create experiences that delight you.

That said, while deciding is simple, it's not always easy.

## WHAT DOES DECIDING REQUIRE?

Deciding requires you to choose a destination.

Are you going to the party? Or not?

Do you want eggs for breakfast? Or a smoothie?

Are you going to publish a book? Or do you hope to publish a book?

Very often, your decision will require subsequent actions in order to manifest. But as we'll discuss shortly, when you're in alignment with your decision, the actions will be obvious and the next logical step on the path.

Your destination can be a specific place (e.g., I will have at least $20,000 reserve in my bank account) or it can be a general feeling (e.g., I am feeling the relief of always knowing that in this exact moment, I have more than enough money) but the act of deciding requires you to feel your desire, allow it, and pay attention to it.

None of this is complex — the unfolding of your life is composed of an endless stream of your decisions, both deliberate and by default. The larger point here is that you need to consciously choose your desires.

The act of choosing (or even imagining) a destination to which you wish to arrive sounds simple enough, but there are several factors that can keep it from being easy.

## WHAT KEEPS US FROM DECIDING?

Why don't we decide our way to our desires?

Well, think of it this way ...

Were you aware that this was how life really worked before?

Probably not.

The idea of deciding to have what you want, and *voila*, it comes into your experience? That's all just a bit too simple, isn't it? To many people this idea falls under the heading of magical thinking. Woo-woo stuff. And in these cases, there's little chance of engaging with the power of deciding in a manner that would reveal its might.

However, because we're indoctrinated with the idea that we need to work, plan, suffer, and wait for the things we really want in life, this isn't surprising. We operate under these assumptions and employ these approaches with varying degrees of success.

But if you're here, you know in your heart there's a better way. And while life may never become easy, by leveraging the power of deciding, it can become easier and filled with more and more moments of sweetness and deeply satisfying creations.

When it comes to the power of deciding, there's an awareness issue — this isn't how we've been conditioned to think about how our lives work. On another level, reducing things to their least common denominator, there are really only two factors at work here: forgetting and fear.

## FORGETTING

Let's review what forgetting means first.

In those moments of anger, sadness, fear, or disappointment — where we feel as though life is not going our way — it's easy to forget that we are the directors of our reality rather than actors being led (or forced) to march down an unwanted path. It's easy to forget that we are always one new decision away from moving in the direction of our desires. And it's often easier to set our power aside and dwell than it is to seize the reins of responsibility to our well-being and harness it.

As basic and fundamental as the power of deciding is, wielding this power to create the outcomes in life that you most desire will always remain a conscious practice. In other words, you need to do the work to see the benefits.

Here's a quick example of what I mean.

Last night I went to bed having closed a lucrative deal with a perfect new client. In the morning I woke to an e-mail informing me that the client had changed her mind and the deal was — POOF! — gone.

Over the first hour of my day, drinking my coffee, my heart filled with disappointment, resentment, and a dollop of self-pity. From a logical point of view, I could brilliantly argue why I was entitled to these feelings. After all, we had an agreement and she broke it.

So, I blamed her for all of my feelings.

In the midst of doing so, my business felt out of my control, like I had to rely on other, unpredictable people (in the form of clients), for my success or failure.

Then I sat down to write this section of the book and the sense of irony took hold.

My inner dialogue sounded like this:

*Oh, yeah. That's right. I'm the director of my reality.*

*I'm the creator of all of it. Okay.*

*Nothing is wrong even though things don't feel good at all.*

But if I want to leverage this contrast to my advantage, it's now my responsibility to decide what it is that I'm wanting from here.

And so, after feeling like a victim of my reality for a while, I remembered that I didn't have to suffer this way. I could decide my way to something more pleasing. So I did. I decided that I would have more cash in my bank account (because that's what this was really about, deep down). And I decided that ALL of my interactions with clients and potential clients are here to help me.

Immediately, I felt the relief of letting go of my resistant thoughts. Then I wrote these paragraphs and went on with my life. Two days later a new client showed up and then another three days later, and then an unexpected mini-windfall from another business I run. And so my desire regarding my bank account came to be and several degrees better than it was before the one deal fell through.

When you live into the practice of deciding and you begin seeing how your manifestations are unmistakable reflections of your conscious decisions, you remember that none of this is magic or a random miracle (though sometimes the unfolding feels magical and miraculous), but rather the inevitable result of deciding what you will have.

But still, at different times and situations, we all forget the power that resides in us, waiting to be leveraged at any moment. While I don't know why we humans are built this way, I believe that part of the reason we forget so much is that it feels so good when you remember. The important thing is to be aware when you're not feeling good and then be vigilant enough about your well-being that you turn your attention to DECIDING.

Because it makes a literal world of difference in what you will experience.

Okay, so one major reason why we fail to decide is because we forget.

The other reason is fear.

## FEAR OF DECIDING

Certainly fear is a blanket term. Really what I am referring to here is the array of uncomfortable feelings that commonly arise when approaching our desires.

So how and why would our desires be connected to unwanted feelings? Seems counterintuitive, right?

Quite simply, as a result of our upbringing and culture, we're conditioned to ignore and suppress our desires. In many cases, we learn to associate having desires with being a selfish, bad person. (I know smart people who flirt with Buddhism, and say things like, "Isn't desire the root of all suffering, though?" No. No it's not.) Naturally, we want to think of ourselves as good so our desires often clash with the beliefs we've taken on to fit into our families and society.

For example, the other day I was taking my family out for a meal at a local restaurant. The entire drive there, my son Alex grumbled from the backseat that he really wanted to go to McDonald's instead. As we were about to enter, I snapped at him, "You're really getting to be a spoiled little boy, aren't you?"

Certainly it pains me to admit that, but it happened and most any parent can relate to this sort of exchange. As parents, our desires will come into conflict with those of our children again and again and sometimes in our being human, things get ugly (and I don't see this dynamic changing anytime soon).

As children, we begin to associate some of our desires with

unpleasant feelings. In this example, I'm quite sure Alex doesn't like to think of himself as selfish or spoiled.

From my son's perspective, he just had a clear desire. He likes Happy Meals. He likes chicken nuggets with lots of ketchup very much, thank you. He likes the little toys in the box. And in that moment, he felt a Happy Meal would make him, well, happy. Period. However, in the face of his clear desire, I sent a powerful message that his audacity to express his desire made him a selfish and bad little person.

Take a moment and think back to your formative years and you'll likely recall several similar personal stories when you were on the receiving end of the message to stifle your desires.

*You should be grateful for what you have.*

*You're really selfish, you know that?*

*Why on Earth do you think you need that?*

*Who do you think you are?*

*Money doesn't grow on trees.*

*You think you're some kind of special, don't you?*

*That seems really risky. What if you're making a mistake?*

*What will "they" think?*

The list is endless, of course.

Those messages that rebuke our desires, that make us feel wrong or doubtful for wanting what we want, have a tendency to seep into our thoughts and infect our beliefs.

Through repetition of exposure to these messages, over time we internalize them and accept them as being the truth. (If you're a parent, in the heat of being in conflict with your child, chances are good you've heard your parents' words come out of your mouth — and then wondered where that came from, right?)

It's worth taking a breath right now and considering some aspect of your life in which you feel like you are struggling to realize your desire (such as relationships, money, well-being, etc.) and see how long it takes you to connect your current experience to a belief you're holding about yourself and that subject. Take it a step further and it's likely you can trace that belief back to a message to which you were repeatedly exposed in your formative years.

In short, in many aspects of our lives, early on we learn to make the association that DESIRE = BAD and this general belief sticks around into adulthood and gets passed down to the next generation.

As adults, it's not usual when new desires pop up from within us that our reflexive response is to start pounding away at them like a game of Whack-a-Mole, to keep them hidden below the surface, so we don't risk the uncomfortable feelings we've learned to associate with simply wanting what we want.

## FEAR OF GETTING IT WRONG

What's another manner in which fear lies at the heart of a failure to decide?

Well, very often it's a fear of making the wrong decision.

But consider this:

What if there weren't any wrong decisions?

Now certainly, there are going to be decisions you make where you don't like the outcome one bit.

But remember, this contrast is just part of the deal of being human. It's the very fuel of every new desire you have, pointing you in the direction of what it is that you want now.

So in a very real sense, you can never make a wrong decision, just decisions you don't like very much.

And yet when we create things we don't like, instead of using the experience to clarify what you're really wanting going forward, often there's a tendency to blame ourselves for having the audacity to ask. Down the road we become wary of desires and stop asking for much.

A friend of mine goes through her life trying to avoid making the wrong decision. It doesn't matter if it's about choosing a parking spot, buying an electric toothbrush, or getting in a relationship with a man.

It's quite clear that she sees her unwanted creations as a reflection of who she is as a person. When things go "wrong" she internalizes this as evidence of her not being smart enough or worthy of her desires.

So when it comes to deciding, she hems and haws. She hesitates. She seeks out everyone else's advice or reads an endless stream of reviews before making a decision. Recently, for weeks she told me of the new car she lusted for, only to settle for a used version of a lesser model, and the problems with the vehicle have already begun.

If any of this sounds (or feels) even a little familiar to you, here's what I want you to consider regarding your decisions.

*What if you really could not get it wrong, ever?*

Because this is the greater truth.

You can't get it wrong. Really.

Certainly, as we discussed a few pages ago, you will always

make decisions that lead to creations you don't like, you will always make "mistakes" — all of this is built in to how our universe of desire and manifestation operate. So when you're trying to avoid creating things you don't like (and you most likely will for all of your days) and you feel the contrast accelerating, this is a good time to remember that you are running a fool's errand, to give up the fight, and remember to decide what you will have going forward.

So, if you're ready to have what you really want, just because you want it, it's time to stop forgetting the power you possess and it's time to stop being guided by fear.

It's time to become someone who DECIDES.

# WHAT DOES DECIDING FEEL LIKE?

REMEMBER that you are deciding continually throughout your waking hours. You have an intention, you line up behind it with no resistance, and it's created.

So the vast majority of your decisions feel like having a piece of toast. You don't think about it very much. You just go to the kitchen, grab the bread, hit a switch, and before you know it — toast!

When the expectation from your desire to manifestation is clear and strong, you give your decision little thought and so usually there's no dramatic (or even noticeable) feelings associated with deciding. This is true even though through the power of these decisions you continually create miracles.

Because when you think about it, having toast on demand really is a miracle.

Consider that right in your home you have an abundance of food, including bread that's already been baked and sliced for you. Then you have a machine specifically designed to cook that bread again into the delightfully specific texture of your choosing. Of course, all of this is powered by the electric current that likely traveled hundreds of miles through a complex series of grids, all the way to your residence, to meet your desires. Along with running water, heating and air conditioning, and wi-fi, and a vehicle that starts when you turn a key or press a button, these are all miracles beyond your personal orchestration or comprehension. So many details of your life go smoothly because you expect them to go smoothly. It's important to remember that *behind each one of those expectations, there's really a decision that you've made with which you stand in alignment and allow.* And because you're not holding any resistant thoughts about the decision, your desires manifest easily.

Paradoxically, when our desires manifest easily, like toast, being able to walk across a room, or the miracle of taking a hot shower, we don't think much about them.

Again, you're already a master decider and a master manifestor. Ninety-nine percent of your desires manifest on demand. However, being human, we tend to focus on the 1% of our desires that have not yet manifested, that seem out of reach.

Right now the simple goal is to remind you to apply this same law of metaphysics to this 1% of your desires and see what unfolds when you consciously enter the practice of deciding to have them.

Here's another way to understand the process of creation: Your decisions manifest because you do not expect them NOT to. Because you don't hold any resistance to the idea of water flowing from your tap, it flows.

So how does it feel when we're tuned into some resistant thoughts associated with our desires?

## WHAT DOES DECIDING NOT FEEL LIKE?

Well, in short, it doesn't feel good.

If this sounds like a simplistic explanation, that's because it is. But again, my job here is to remind you of how simple and immediately accessible the process and power of deciding really is.

So when you don't feel good about something — you're feeling the contrast of what you DON'T WANT — this is your indicator that you're not fully leveraging your contrast to help you decide. In these situations, it's your job to actively tune the receiver to where the signal is strong and clear. Where there's resistance, deciding requires your conscious focus.

For example, yesterday I spoke to my accountant about our yearly taxes. I was expecting a rebate (or at least to owe nothing), but it turned out that we'd need to make a payment to the government of several thousand dollars.

My initial response was frustration and anger. I had enough money to pay the bill, but had planned on putting these dollars toward something fun. I spent an hour or so blaming my accountant and ranting to my wife, and feeling rather sorry for myself. In short, to anyone observing me, I played the role of victim at a Daytime Emmy-winning level.

I had temporarily forgotten the power that always resides within me. I had forgotten that I get to decide how it all goes in my life. I had forgotten that I direct the flow of money into my life and that no entity outside myself determines my outcomes. I had forgotten that the purpose of this unwanted experience was to help me clarify an updated and revised version of my desires. I had temporarily forgotten that my feeling bad was my indicator that in this moment, I was bleeding out my power by not making a decision as to what I truly wanted to create in my life going forward.

But with some time and a few deep breaths (and working on this book), I remembered.

I could see that this creation, *my creation*, was giving me a perfect opportunity to decide what it is that I wanted going forward.

So what do I want?

In the larger picture of things, I want everything in my life to be paid for, easily.

More specifically, I want to sit on the deck of my beautiful new little cabin in the woods, appreciating the magnificent view with a good friend or two, and laughing over a couple of beers. This is what I really wanted the money for.

Now the moment I connect to these thoughts and *I decide that these desires are mine now by FEELING them now*, my work is done.

I've decided what I will have and that's that. In this *decision*, I allow myself to feel the presence of my desire in my life in this moment, even before it's physically manifested. Simply put, this feels good. It feels like relief. It feels like ease.

As long as I don't get in my own way and exercise some patience through expectant anticipation, my desires will be mine through the awesome power of deciding. That's how it works. Every time and without exception.

After making this decision *that everything works out for me, always*, with some back and forth with my accountant, we discovered that by contributing more money to my retirement account (something I intended to do but had forgotten) instead of just paying the government, I was able to both invest money toward the future and completely eliminate my tax liability for the year.

(As a side note, I invested in a stock I'd been looking at for a while but never bought. The price just happened to be at its low price for the year and within two months, I made a 20% return on the investment. *Everything works out for me, always*.)

Certainly my point isn't about advising you on your taxes, but rather illustrating that when you leverage contrast to DECIDE how you wish to feel and the general course you want your life to take, the road rises to meet you in very satisfying and unexpected ways. This is the magic of deciding.


## DECIDING FEELS BETTER

Okay, so let's go back to the original question as to what deciding feels like?

When you've made a decision that is in alignment with your desires, *deciding feels better*.

Notice that *deciding doesn't always feel good*. Sometimes none of the options that we see in front of us feel *good*, especially when we're at the bottom of an emotional hole. But there is always an option that *feels better*, even if it's only a few inches in the direction of where we want to go.

And when it comes to deciding, it's critical to remember to *pay attention to what feels better, rather than what looks better*.

For example, years ago, after my father's death, my four siblings and I had to decide how to care for my Alzheimer's-stricken mother. There were no options that felt good in front of us. The decision to place my mother in an assisted-living facility felt "less bad" than the other unattractive options. But

35

less bad is still better, a rung or two higher on the ladder of emotions.

My mother lived in this nursing home for several years. As she continued to deteriorate, my visits with her became more difficult. They were never satisfying in any way. I'd reached the point where I felt worse after every visit. I realized that the only reason I visited was to protect myself from being haunted by the guilt of not visiting her. After all, the norms of polite society dictated that a son not visiting his beloved mother wouldn't *look right*.

But after one particular visit, I sat in the parking lot, feeling the contrast of another depressing experience at the nursing home. I took a few breaths and remembered to leverage the power of deciding by asking myself, "What would feel better to me right now?"

The answer felt very clear. I never wanted to return to this facility. And I also realized how long I'd been ignoring the truth of this feeling, allowing my decisions to be made by the default fear what "they" would think about me. Sitting in my car that afternoon, I summoned the courage to decide to follow what felt a little better to me.

I never went back to that nursing home for the last year or so of my mother's life. While this decision may not have looked right on the surface, it felt better to me and I never even had a whiff of regret. (For the record, I began visiting my mom again near the end of her life when she was transferred to another facility, and it felt better to do so.)

## DECIDING SOMETIMES FEELS LIKE RELIEF

When you're leveraging the power of contrast as in the previous example of my mother, in these cases, deciding feels like *relief*.

Relief doesn't always equate to feeling *good*, but it's a clear indicator that you're now heading down a path that's aligned with your deeper desire.

This relief comes from the fact that you're making the conscious decision to go with your own flow, to drop your resistance, and align yourself with what you really want (instead of staying stuck focusing of what you don't want, or trying to will yourself into alignment with someone else's plan).

Likewise, when you make a decision that's not in alignment with your desires (or you fail to make a new decision in response to an unwanted experience), you will feel worse.

Remember, your job is to direct your reality through your decisions as to what you will have. If you find yourself feeling the churn of worry about some aspect of your future, this feeling is your cue to step into the relief of deciding and directing.

## DECIDING FEELS LIKE CERTAINTY

In winter, I heat our home with a wood stove. Every autumn, I handle several cords of firewood and split a lot of logs.

After standing a log on the chopping stump, I look at the grain of the wood and focus on where my ax will fall.

In that focusing, I have made my decision.

Much of the time, I am so certain with the outcome that the ax falls where I intend and the wood splits into two satisfying, clean halves.

However, if the log is especially dense or filled with knots, I begin to contemplate where and how to strike.

Seeds of doubt take root in my head. I begin to wonder, "Hmmm ... Am I going to be able to get through this thing?"

And when I wonder how (or if I can) split the wood, I have not made a decision. I've not cut off other possibilities in my mind.

In these cases, usually the feedback is immediate. The moment my ax hits the wood it jumps back at me, stinging my hands. The same principle is involved in martial arts where people split boards or concrete blocks with their hands. With enough experience, it becomes clear that the splitting takes place in the mind before the hand or ax touches the object.

Some pieces of wood prove too tough to split. When this happens, I simply toss them aside instead of tiring myself out. The same is true for the decisions you're not ready to make.

If you have a desire and you find yourself hoping, wondering, curious, worried, or uncertain whether this desire will manifest, you've made a choice, but you're not deciding in a manner to deliberately create the outcome you want. In these cases, you can expect to feel your hands stinging — there will be some clear feedback that you haven't really decided.

It's your responsibly to feel the feedback and to recognize it as your creation, one that is trying to guide you to make a new decision.

while the light burns Green, there will be a flicker of doubt as you come up against an old thought.

Personally, I notice that when I make a higher ticket purchase, even though I am certain of what I want and am aligned with this thing (my house, a new vehicle, The View, etc.) and the Green Light is shining, some resistant thoughts pop up like weeds.

In the case of buying something, usually these thoughts reflect some old personal beliefs related to money.

*If I buy this thing that I really want, will I have enough later?*

*Do I really need this thing (that I really want), or can I do without it?*

*What if (this bad thing happens to me)?*


## GREEN LIGHTS STILL REQUIRE COURAGE

But in order to experience the *fun* and *freedom* of deciding, you must have the courage to follow what you *feel* instead of what you *think*.

This is the critical distinction upon which all of your outcomes lie.

When you feel the Green Light, the YES of your desires, then it's your job to allow yourself to go with your desires and let the Universe sort out the details. The fun and freedom of deciding comes from watching the pieces fall into place after you fully step into your desire.

The reason your "big" desire isn't showing up is because you entertain thoughts that run counter to your belief that you can have this "big" thing that you want. "Big" is in quotes because to the Universe, creating a single dollar is the same as creating millions of them — the only relevant factor is the degree to which you decide and allow yourself to have what you ask for.

The fact that we don't always decide to have some of our desires right away is no big deal. In fact it's perfectly natural as you wouldn't want to manifest ALL your desires at once — where would you put it all? And as your desires emerge and evolve, you'll always experience some contrast and resistance. Just part of the game we all came here to play.

So before you can really leverage the power of deciding to create some desire that feels like it's been eluding you, it's important to remember that being a master of deciding requires you to live from courage.

Courage (from the Latin root, *cor* — meaning the heart) means you must start living from your heart. You must allow the desires within you to surface, release your judgment around having them, and then allow them to come into your experience.

When you live from your heart, you allow yourself to pay attention to what you feel in your body and you give this information priority over your thoughts or the prevailing wisdom of the culture as to what's possible.

Very often this will require you to tap into your courage, to swat aside the mental mosquitoes of your old nagging doubts, and to honor what feels right to you and to take the leap. Living from your heart often feels like a radical act for the simple fact that your life will not look like anyone else's.

But again, this is nothing new for you. Think back to your life and you'll be able to pull out instances where you felt the Green Light, trusted your inner knowing, and you felt your awesome superpower of creating your desires through your decisions. Leverage your memories and follow your courage.

## YELLOW LIGHTS MEAN WAIT

It's okay to wait until you know.

I wanted The View from the first moment I saw it over a decade ago.

However, for all that time, the light was Yellow, not Green.

As clear as my desire was, there were no next steps that felt like a Green Light. Instead, every time I thought about what to do next, or I'd devise some plan to acquire the property, I felt overwhelmed with the complexity of my ideas.

Any action I considered taking felt like stepping on the accelerator to race though a Yellow Light before it turned Red at a blind intersection.

As much as I wanted my light to be Green, it was Yellow.

So I did nothing beyond visiting the property and appreciating it for over twelve years because there was nothing clear for me to do.

Remember that when you're leveraging the power of deciding and allowing by playing Red Light/Green Light, manifestation will feel like it's unfolding for you. You'll never feel like you're forcing an outcome, trying to jam a puzzle piece into a space that *almost* fits.

I don't pretend to know why the timing of things is the way it is. But I do know that if you have a desire within you, and you decide to have it, it will be yours. You just might have to remain patient and certain in your desire and wait for the light to turn Green.

You'll know that the light has turned Green when any subsequent actions just feel like the clear, obvious thing to do.

Oftentimes the most powerful strategy to getting what you really want is to respect your Yellow Lights by being willing to wait until you *know*. No one or no entity holds the power to make you override your inner guidance. Trust yourself. If you cannot get to the place where you feel fully aligned before making your decision, wait.

Decide that right now is not the time for you decide.


## BE WILLING TO FAIL

At first glance, the notion that being willing to fail might seem at odds with what we've been talking about — being bold and powerfully declaring what you will have.

But it's not.

When you talk to people about their biggest dreams and ask them what holds them back in their pursuit of these desires, far and away, the most common answer is a fear of failure.

This isn't surprising when you consider how we're conditioned from the earliest ages socially and institutionally to internalize failure as the worst possible outcome. Failure means we're bad. Failure means we did it wrong. Failure means we're less than. Failure, especially in public, is humiliating. The list goes on, but we learn to fear failure quickly and go to lengths to avoid experiencing it.

But here's the rub.

The Universe operates vibrationally.

What you feel is what you get.

What you get is what you feel.

So when you're operating from a place where you're not

wanting (or more specifically, willing) to fail, a couple of things are happening in the background.

First, you're likely setting the bar of your dreams too close to the ground. In other words, you're likely asking for what you believe you can get easily, the fruit that's already hanging low, rather than deciding to have what you'd really, really enjoy experiencing. And you only get what you allow yourself to have, so this approach doesn't allow you to flex the muscles that come standard with your superpower to decide.

Second, approaching your desires with the dominant thought of "don't fail" — an outcome that you DON'T WANT — is the vibrational equivalent of informing the vibrationally-powered Universe to show you failure.

If you're a sports fan, you've likely seen the phenomenon of a team playing not to lose instead of playing to win. Typically, this happens late in a game where an underdog has a lead over a favorite. As the underdog becomes aware that they're getting closer to an improbable victory, they stop being aggressive and start playing cautiously. When this happens, it's very common for the underdog to begin making all sorts of unforced errors, and in turn, the favorite comes away with the win.

The better approach is to play to win. At its core, playing to win means that you are *willing* to lose.

When you are willing to lose, the specter of failure loses its power over you. When you no longer resist the idea of what you DON'T WANT, you swing open the door fully to what you DO WANT.

To be clear, being willing to fail does not mean that you welcome failure or that you expect it. Rather it means that you can entertain the outcome of not having something that you want, and BE OKAY with it. Not pretending to be pleased, of course. But not crushed, either. In this way, you're dropping your resistance to anything unwanted and become a more open conduit to manifesting your desire.

## DO THE WORK OF IMAGINING

At the root of all deciding lies desire.

Before you can decide your way to something that you want, first you must imagine what it is that what you want to create.

Now you're always imagining, you're always using your thoughts to create images in your mind, and those images are the precise blueprints for all of your life's creations.

Years ago I read Wallace Wattles' classic book, *The Science of Getting Rich*. Paraphrasing him, he wrote that all the Universe was made of "thinking stuff," and that your thoughts make impressions on this thinking stuff, and those impressions then cause your thoughts to take form in the world. I always imagined this thinking stuff to be like a big marshmallow and my thoughts are like a hot branding iron that takes the exact shape of that thought and burns it into the marshmallow. That impression from the iron — our decision as to what we will have — is then created for us and held in a waiting room until we're aligned with it enough to allow it to come into our experience.

A current analogy would be to look at how 3-D printers do a mind-bending job of turning thoughts into manifested form. These machines can create anything from a cup, to a house, to a human body part. In order to create an object from a 3-D printer, first that object must begin with the thought of what to create. What you imagine and then program into the software determines exactly what the printer will create. Of course, the Universe creates on your behalf in the exact same manner. It

What if all goes smoothly with rebooking our rental car and hotel? What if this is all part of the adventure with the kids? What if this is all for the best?"

As I entertained those thoughts, I immediately felt a wave of relief wash over me. My stress sweat dried. My breathing slowed. While the people next to me continued to focus on how their future plans were ruined, I used my imagination to start forming the pictures of the outcomes I wanted when it was my turn to speak to the airline representative.

When it was my turn, the rep had bad news.

"There's not another flight with available seats out of here until Sunday evening," she said.

By the time we'd arrive, this would eat three days of our vacation and many dollars worth of non-refundable contracts.

"We're going to need another option," I replied, as I imagined my family gathering on the beach to watch the sunset. I had no clue what was on her screen, but I had decided this was all working out.

After several minutes of her clacking keys, she had seats on a flight at another airport about two hours away early the next morning. Did we want it?

We did. As we drove, we booked a hotel room located right inside the airport. The trip began to feel like a family bonding experience of us co-navigating through shared adversity. When we arrived, the hotel had a swimming pool so my kids were thrilled. However, in all the commotion of finding another flight, it hadn't dawned on me that our return flight tickets would still be taking us back to Albany, New York, even though we were now departing and leaving our vehicle 120 miles away in Connecticut.

While the kids were swimming I went down to the check-in counter at the new airport. The rep greeted me with a stone-face as I explained the situation and how we needed return tickets to Connecticut now. I held up the line for twenty minutes as she clacked keys, made phone calls, and generally expressed her displeasure of having to deal with me. In my mind, I let her be where she was at and the situation be what it was and just kept my focus on the beach. We'd be there soon enough and in a moment when all this was over, I'd grab a seat at the bar and enjoy a cold beer.

"Okay, I spoke with my manager and we can change your flight. However, the only available seats are a direct flight on Saturday as Friday is completely booked," she said coldly without looking up from her screen.

"That would be just fine, thank you," I said, feeling the warmth of another fulfilled intention wash through me. I used my imagination to picture what I wanted to create, and I basked in the moment of its arrival.

As she handed me the boarding passes for the returning flight, I couldn't wait to find my wife and share the experience because deciding your way through life is fun. In the end, my family enjoyed better weather, we had another evening on the beach to soak in another sunset, and we now had the time for a lovely celebratory meal with our friends that we otherwise would have not seen for another year.

From one perspective, a couple of changed flights would fail to qualify as miraculous. However, from another perspective, everything that took place here was a miracle. Everything that happened followed my imagination's lead. Every action that was taken, and every unfolding, came from the decision to follow what felt better and felt obvious in the moment.

The real point here is that the quality of your life is dependent on the degree to which you consciously direct your imagination in alignment with your desires. What's more, through your superpower of deciding, in any given moment, you are holding the keys as to what experience you will have in any area of your life.

## PART 1 - DECIDE - SUMMARY

When I first saw The View, I felt the rush of desire move through me.

"I want this," I thought.

And on one important level, it was done.

However, even though I was clear in my desire, I wasn't in alignment with having it yet.

In short, the thought of having it in that moment felt overwhelming to me. At first, the property wasn't even for sale and then when it did come on the market, the price felt way out of my range.

While many decisions lead to nearly instant manifestation, some decisions — especially the ones that stretch your current boundaries and beliefs as to what's possible for you — take time for all the necessary conditions to appear and organize in order to manifest.

Here's how it works.

When you decide upon something that you want, in that moment, on a metaphysical level, the fulfillment of that desire is indeed created for you in energetic form and waiting for you to become a match to receive it. Abraham-Hicks refers to this as your desire waiting for you in *vibrational escrow*. However, for that escrow to come into your personal account, your reality, you must be the embodiment of that which you've asked for (e.g., you cannot experience well-being in your body if your focus is always on thoughts of what's wrong with your health).

For this reason, the second essential element of the process of deciding requires you to ALIGN with your decision.

# PART II
# ALIGN

# THE VIEW STORY PART II: ALIGN

*"The property up top sold, you know?"*

*My neighbor Al's words surprised me like quick jab to the cheek.*

*While we'd shared stories of our mutual appreciation for The View, I never shared with him the depth of how connected I felt to this parcel of land.*

*Al went on to fill me in on the backstory, and that the newly retired couple in their mid-60s would be moving in the July 4th weekend.*

*I returned home, thinking that was it regarding my dream (it had always been just a little fantastical, a little too far out of my league, hadn't it?) and decided to hope for the best from my new neighbor.*

*Two weeks later, I met the new buyer, Rich, as I was mowing my lawn at the intersection of our properties at the top of the hill. We felt each other out as we discussed where our property boundaries lay and how a right-of-way we now shared worked.*

*I asked him about his decision to move to the area, and, predictably, he cited the view from his new home. Pointing beyond his home to the hedgerow that marks the entrance to The View, I agreed with him.*

*"I've always said that your new view over in that field is simply the best in the area."*

*"Oh, yes," he answered, his tone shifting.*

*"Well, ah ... we didn't buy those three acres. Not now, anyway. Probably buy 'em a little later," he said.*

*Rich kept speaking for a few more minutes, but I did not hear a word he said.*

*Did he say that The View is a separate plot of land?*

*Did he say that he didn't buy it?*

*I shook his hand and pointed my lawn tractor down the hill to our house. I ran inside and flew to my computer.*

*Accessing the county tax map, sure enough, The View lay on a separate three-acre plot of land. I'd never realized this before because the seller only offered both plots as a single package.*

*Apparently, because the house was on the market so long, the sellers chose to close on the bigger deal of the home and twenty acres, and offer the other three acres – The View – separately.*

*My whole body vibrated. Hummed, really. Tingles shot up and down my spine just like when I hear a song I love. The decision I'd made long ago to have this property was now coming into focus and I felt a part of the unfolding in real time.*

*And it was absolutely glorious.*

*Before I could think about anything, I Googled the real estate agent who sold the home to Rich, called and introduced myself. I asked about the three acres and he said, yes, it would be going on the market shortly. He even agreed to give me the first shot at it.*

*More tingles. More knowing.*

*From my office, I ran upstairs and told my wife how The View was on a separate plot of land and was still available.*

*"Can you believe it?" I said.*

*And yes, she could believe it. She was happy for me of course — mostly because I was so excited, but her enthusiasm didn't touch mine.*

*After all, this was my dream. Not hers. She appreciated The View too, of course. But quite simply, this property felt connected to my DNA in ways that went beyond the aesthetics.*

*I had no idea what the asking price would be, but I came up with a few educated guesses and pulled out my calculator. I decided I would find a way to make this work.*

*From that moment on, I told everyone I knew (whom I thought might "get it" in terms of manifesting a big dream) the story of The View being on the market and how things felt like they were lining up for me.*

*A few people looked at me and politely nodded, unable to connect to the feeling I offered in the telling of the story. I didn't really care though, because I was telling the story for me, getting myself more and more behind my decision to have it.*

*With every telling, I could feel the momentum swelling.*

---

*MY FRIEND CHRIS and I had just shed our bags in our Toronto hotel room for a concert when my phone buzzed. I recognized the number as Bob the realtor and I knew he'd be contacting me to relay the asking price for The View.*

*Too nervous to hear the number, I let the call go. A moment later my phone beeped with the voicemail.*

*Adrenaline pumping, I listened to the message. The polite voice informed me that the sellers were asking more than double the price of what I'd hoped for: $50,000.*

*Shit. Now what?*

*I called Bob back and thanked him for giving me the first shot at the property. I told him of my surprise at the price, given that land is relatively cheap where we live and that its assessed value was half that, at which he replied, "Yes, but the view ..."*

*For the first time, I felt the place slipping away from me. As I was about to hang up I told him I would be in touch if I ever felt like I could make an offer close to the asking price.*

*"Okay," he said. "Just keep in mind a cash offer tends to go a long way ..." and with those final words, I felt a sense of possibility again, a wink of an opening.*

*I relayed the conversation to Chris.*

*He heard the mix of excitement and doubt in my voice.*

*He didn't offer a word of advice, but rather raising his beer can to mine offered a three-word toast:*

*"It's yours, dude."*

*His simple gesture, his belief in and for me, allowed me to instantly realign with my courage. Like a good coach, he held my dream in a space of certainty — this is a done deal and you know it, Drew — and this allowed me to set aside my doubts and instead bask in the wonderful feeling that I had the power to have exactly what I wanted.*

*Chris and I clinked our cans in celebration and went to our concert to celebrate some more.*

# WHAT DOES IT MEAN TO ALIGN?

THE SECOND ESSENTIAL element of the deciding process requires you to Align.

In order to deliberately create your reality through the power of deciding, you must maintain a consistent sense of vibrational alignment with your decision. In other words, if you imagine something you want and you decide to have it, you then must maintain your belief that it's on the way to you. When deciding what you will have, you can't be wishy-washy, doubtful, or half-assed and expect it to show up. Rather, you must decide and then take on the responsibility of seeing your decision through to fruition.

In basketball there's an old saying, "The ball goes where the wrist flows" to emphasize the critical nature of following through to hit your target. Using this analogy, where deciding is the act of taking a shot, aligning is the act of having your wrist fully follow through towards the basket after you release the ball. Likewise, after you decide, very often your desire will not appear instantly, especially if you have some inner resistance to the idea that you can really have something that you want. In these instances, you'll need to enter the practice of aligning yourself by consistently choosing thoughts that support your decision.

For another practical analogy, think about when you get your car aligned. Ideally when you're driving in a straight line and you take your hands off the wheel, all the weight of your vehicle and the steering assembly are tuned and balanced in such a way that your vehicle continues to move in that straight line. Likewise when you're completely aligned with a decision you've made, the path to manifesting your desire is a straight line.

However, if you notice that your vehicle drifts to the left or right when you let go of the wheel, a technician makes adjustments to restore balance and eliminate resistance.

In order to deliberately create your reality through the power of deciding, you must be in alignment with your decision and very often this requires you to tweak some of your thoughts and feelings after you decide to stay on course to manifestation.

# WHAT DOES ALIGNING FEEL LIKE?

IN THE PROCESS of leveraging the power of deciding, aligning is where much of the heavy lifting takes place. This is where you need to be actively aware of your thoughts and consciously direct them.

So what does the process of aligning feel like?

Aligning feels like calibrating.

Aligning feels like getting up and moving your chair around a campfire to keep the smoke out of your eyes.

Aligning feels like lying on mattress after mattress in the show-room, looking for the one that feels just right to you and being patient enough to find it, even if you have to walk away.

Here's the gist of alignment: I love to ski. At the same time, I'm crowd-averse. The thought of competing for parking or walking long distances across multiple parking lots lugging bulky, heavy ski gear fills me with dread. This is exactly what I DON'T want, yet on the weekends when I ski with my kids, the resorts tend to be very busy places.

However, as someone who delights in practicing the art of creating my own personal reality, circumstances be damned, years ago I decided that when it comes to finding the perfect parking spot close to the lodge and lifts, no matter the situation before me, I will be triumphant.

And with this decision, like magic, this is what has been.

I can't count the times that I have pulled up to the resort with an employee with a flag, waving me to park in Siberia Lot, a half-mile from the lodge. Instead of following this suggestion, I offer the attendant a smile and a wave indicating that I'm dropping off our gear at the lodge, and proceed past the LOT FULL sign to the area adjacent to the lodge. In that moment, even though the place is jammed, I'm not driving with a sense of hope like one *hopes* to win the lottery. I'm driving with a sense of expectant anticipation, a certainty that despite the apparent odds, the perfect parking spot awaits me.

To be clear, there is no rational reason for me to expect there to be an open parking space. Most of the skiers accept this and just follow the man with the flag and walk. But when it comes to parking spots, I've decided I'm special, that I possess this super-power. And that's that.

Now it may take a few minutes of going up and down the rows of vehicles, and there may be other crafty drivers on the prowl with me, but almost without fail, someone will appear with keys in hand, opening up their spot for me. I remember one day, the most crowded I'd ever seen the resort, thousands of cars jammed every lot by the time that I arrived. People were parking so far away they needed to take a shuttle just to reach the mountain. Me? I proceeded past the masses and pulled into the third-closest parking spot in the entire resort. Magic.

These events delight me to no end because in that moment, I

feel my connection to my superpower to decide what I will have. This is always just a lovely feeling to remember.

Here's where the process of aligning comes in.

Even though from the moment I leave my house I've decided that I'm going to find the perfect parking spot no matter what, and even though I have a long history of being successful, I start off feeling quite anxious. I worry about finding a spot. I start thinking about how much of a hassle it's going to be to walk or wait for a shuttle. In short, my default thinking is not in alignment with my desire. If I remain focused on what I DON'T WANT, that is what I will get. (Yes, every once in a while I get skunked and find myself doing the long walk.)

However, my usual habit is that the closer we get to the mountain, the more I recalibrate my thoughts. When we're a few miles away, I start to visualize the spot. I remind myself that this is my superpower. I even imagine myself not finding a close spot, having to walk, and being okay with this thought (this drops my resistance to WHAT I DON'T WANT). By deliberately connecting to all of these thoughts instead of my default thoughts of worry and anxiousness, I am doing the work of alignment.

Whether your desire is parking spaces, a specific dollar amount in your bank account, or attracting a life partner, the same rules apply. Decide to have what you want. Then look inward to make sure that you are choosing thoughts that allow you to feel into the certainty of your desire being on its way to you.

## WHAT DOES ALIGNING REQUIRE?

Alignment requires you to be a match for what it is that you've decided you want.

If you're a match for your desire (that is, you don't hold any resistance to the idea of having it), it's yours, end of story. Again this how the vast majority of your decisions manifest themselves almost instantly.

However, when you're not a current match for something you want (that is, your current beliefs about your desire do not line up with the feeling of having that desire), you'll need to get into alignment in order to see your desire.

There's a Kurt Vonnegut quote that sums up my beliefs as to what the process of aligning requires. It goes like this:

*"Another flaw in the human character is that everybody wants to build and nobody wants to do maintenance."*

Whereas deciding requires you to imagine the destination you wish to reach, getting into alignment with a desire you're currently not a match for requires you to do the work that puts you in tune with reaching that destination. In the process of deciding, aligning is where the most work takes place.

More specifically, aligning requires you to be conscious, deliberate, and vigilant regarding the thoughts you are choosing to put your attention on.

When it comes to real world manifestation, it's the practice of alignment that separates those who realize their dreams from those who pine away for them because a decision without alignment is just a wish.

## WHAT KEEPS US FROM ALIGNING?

Just as you are a master of deciding, you are also a master of aligning. You course-correct, adjust, and fine-tune so often, you tend not to notice that you're doing it. For example, if you're taking a portrait photo and the subject's eyes are closed in the shot, you take another to get the desired image. When you hop in the shower and the water feels too hot, you adjust the dial. If you're really unhappy in your relationship, you make changes or go your separate ways. These are all forms of aligning with your desires, and again, you engage in this process countless times, every day of your life.

However, even though our personal experiences show us that aligning with our desires leads to the manifestations we want, we don't always engage in the conscious practice of aligning, especially when it comes to some of our deeper desires.

So this begs the question ...

If deciding truly is our innate superpower that works every single time we apply it, why do we fail to spend much time practicing alignment?

Because we're not taught about the power of our thoughts, it follows that most of us never build the habit of taking the time to deliberately choose aligned thoughts. Like working out, meditating, or journaling, the practice of alignment requires you to take a time out from the busyness of life and turn your focus inward. Instead of passively consuming, aligning requires you to consciously create. Aligning is most definitely work, and it can seem like one more thing to do in a life bulging with daily tasks, though the greater point of this book is to remind you that the return on investment for this work is unparalleled.

Also, let's not discount the fact that the dominant cultural belief is that success is more dependent on what you DO compared to what you THINK. Personally, I spent twenty years in school — all the way through to earning a Ph.D. — and at no time did a counselor, teacher, or mentor make single reference to the idea that I could decide my way to my desires. My elementary school-age kids come home with reams of worksheets to prove that they can follow the formulas handed to them, but the thought of any inner work remains a foreign (if not frivolous) concept in the curriculum.

Even if you're a believer in the power of deliberate creation, this is so deeply engrained that when you're thinking about your dreams and whether you can really decide your way to having them, there's likely a part of you that's thinking, "Yeah, but ..." And this is to be expected given what we were taught.

I include myself here. Even though I've experienced the magic of deciding countless times over the course of my life, even with a long personal history of how things have turned out far better that anything I'd planned when I decided and let go, I still forget the power of aligning. Instead, I fall back to the deeply engrained and cheaper habits of working harder, or worrying, or complaining.

However, when I get around to choosing the thought that I can simply decide to have things go my way, I feel a sense of relief. It's my reminder that aligning my thoughts with the outcome I desire is the most important, most efficient, and most powerful thing I can do.

You'll know that this approach is for you if the mere thought of deciding what you want feels better than your current approach. However, there's only one way to experience the power of aligning and that is to put this theoretical concept into practice. (It's worth noting that every critic to a metaphysical approach does so from the sidelines, trying to poke holes in the theory with what-about-isms. They don't do the conscious work of deciding and aligning and then judging from their own results.)

So, can you really decide to have parking spaces appear? Can you decide that the lover you desire will find their way to your bed? Can you decide to have the dollars that you want to appear in your bank account? Can you decide to live a life where you're healthy and feel good in your body until the day you die? Can you decide your way to having your dream property fall into your lap?

The truth is that you'll never know the true depth of your superpower of deciding until you start applying it in areas and ways that you may not have considered before. And no, you'll never do this perfectly. But keep this critical point in mind — whatever you choose to decide and align with, you are always right.

## ALIGNMENT REQUIRES YOU TO REMEMBER THAT YOU ARE ALWAYS RIGHT

You've likely heard the pithy Henry Ford quote that sums up this next point.

*"If you think you can do a thing or think you can't do a thing, you're right."*

Not only can you not get your decisions wrong, but you are always RIGHT.

But we need to remember (and this is the whole purpose of this book) that no one, no entity, and no circumstance is ever responsible for the direction your life takes. You're always sitting in the driver's seat of this big bus called Life.

The Universe follows *your* lead. That's how it works. Contrary to common belief, the Universe is not playing a metaphysical game of hide-and-seek with you, offering you occasional signs to follow like trail markers in a forest to guide you to your destination. Now, it's certainly possible (and often delightful) to experience signs, but they appear as a result of your direction.

Signs appear because *you decided* you wanted to see signs. The Universe has no interest in leading you anywhere or to any right destination, because there is none. Rather, like an impeccable butler, the Universe is simply fulfilling your assertions as to what you will have.

So you get what you decide to have through the direction of your thoughts. Always. With this superpower comes the responsibility to care for it. And you care for it by doing the hard work of choosing thoughts that align with your decisions and desires.

Ford had another quote that speaks to this element of deciding.

*"Thinking is the hardest work there is, which is probably the reason why so few engage in it."*

If you want to see your life change as the result of your decisions, do the work of getting into alignment and directing your thoughts so you can unlock the magic.

I have a friend who's constantly posting about relationships — his desire to be in a healthy one with a woman is very strong. And yet most of his posts are about how the last woman he dated wronged him and how women cannot be trusted. He proclaims what a good guy he is, expressing a genuine sense of bewilderment as to how yet another relationship fell apart. After a few months when he enters a new relationship, he'll start posting how this one is *the one*, and detail how in love he feels. But over the past two decades, things always unfold the same way. Within a few months, there's another messy breakup. He ends up unable to fathom how or why he's been so unfairly treated once again.

While this person lives in pain and frustration, he does not yet see is that he is always right. His dominant beliefs — the thoughts he's deciding to focus on — are that he cannot find what he's looking for no matter how hard he tries, and that he needs to protect himself from getting hurt. And so due to the nature of how our decisions manifest themselves in our lives, he is proven right time and time again. While the women's identities change, the characteristics of each of the relationships play out as if they're all following the exact same script.

A tricky thing here is that he's making his decisions about women from past experiences and indeed, he may have stacks of evidence to prove his case that his assertions are true. But going back to the fundamental leap that allows us to leverage the superpower of deciding, he's not yet taken on the role of the creator of his reality, so he's taking the much less successful path of deciding by default. He won't see the power of his decisions until he aligns himself with the power of deciding.

Here are a few points worth noting. Just as my friend keeps making decisions from his past experiences, when it comes to living into the power of deciding, remember that while the past might be *interesting*, it's not the slightest bit *relevant* to how you direct your reality. What you choose and align yourself with NOW is all that matters.

Second, keep in mind that it's impossible to be in a place of blame and be in alignment with your desires. You know blame is not aligned because blaming always feels worse than not blaming. Certainly you will fall into the trap of blaming people and circumstances (including yourself) as you move through your life. The key is to notice when you're blaming and then do the work of directing your thoughts in line with your intentions.

Living in alignment requires you to respect the fact that you are always right in regard to what you assert to be true.

## ALIGNING REQUIRES YOU TO GET BEHIND YOUR DECISION

Most of the time when we're consciously thinking about a decision, it's regarding something that we're not 100% certain on.

*Should I stay or should I go?*

*Is this the right color to paint the wall?*

*Should I buy this house? Or the other one?*

Why is it critical to get behind your decision?

Because even though you cannot ever get a decision wrong, you will always be proven right. If you fail to get behind your decision, you will likely be dissatisfied with what you create.

This is because the magic of consciously directing your desires through deciding does not come from making a right decision versus a wrong one. Instead, the magic is a perfect reflection of the degree of your *alignment* with the decision you make.

Getting behind your decisions is another way of getting into alignment that often requires your focus and effort.

To my perfectionist friends out there, you'll do yourself a favor by releasing your conditioning and embracing the truth that there are no right decisions and there are no wrong decisions. Instead, there are decisions you get behind and support that manifest more quickly in ways that please you. And there are decisions you fail to get behind and support that manifest more slowly (if at all), and in ways that tend to please you less.

Again, you will always make decisions that lead to outcomes you don't like. But remember that all of those outcomes are your creations, all of which exist to serve you. Certainly in the midst of feeling the disappointment or frustration of not getting what you want, embracing this idea can be tough.

But leveraging your superpower of deciding requires you to gulp it down and begin seeing how the things that don't look or feel like they are working out are indeed helping you move toward your desires through the clarity that contrast provides.

However, while contrasting experiences are an inevitable ingredient of life, we want our decisions to lead to the best outcomes.

So, in the practice of deciding, what's the best way to always make the right decision?

The best way to make decisions that consistently lead to the outcomes you want is to *consciously get behind any decision you make.*

Your decision is like a boxer in the ring. You're the corner person. Your job is to support your fighter, to create a vision of victory, to have your decision's back and to champion it in every way.

However, if you think, "Wow, this guy looks really tough to beat. Let's hope you don't get hurt out there ..." you're not getting behind your decision. You've cut your own desire down at the knees.

A friend of mine recently posted his experience about buying a new mattress. It was very detailed, encouraging you to bring your own sheets to the store, to lie on each one you try for at least thirty minutes in the showroom, and so on. He revealed he'd spent many hours in this process, including buying and returning three mattresses.

It was clear from reading his words that his desire to buy the right mattress was very strong (after all, this was an expensive purchase, he reasoned). But it was equally clear that instead of getting into alignment with his desire and deciding, he allowed his focus to weigh more heavily on NOT wanting to make the mistake of buying the wrong mattress.

Instead of powerfully directing his reality through the magic of deciding and then backing his decision, he tentatively backed his decision by hoping it would work out. When you operate this way, from a metaphysical perspective, you are planning to create an unwanted outcome.

(Without getting behind his decision, he expressed how he wasn't particularly pleased with his fourth mattress purchase either.)

I couldn't help but compare my friend's experience to my mattress-buying experience. My wife and I wanted a comfortable king bed. We did not consider what might not go right. We were just excited about getting something new and nice. We expected things to go well and so they did. We went in the store, hopped on a few mattresses, found a clear winner, and bought it. I know that every night I get into bed, I notice myself appreciating how wonderful and comfortable it is.

Whether we're talking about mattresses, money markets, or marriage partners, failing to get behind your decision and the wishy-washy results that follow are commonplace. However, things can go much easier when you consciously make a decision and simply get behind that decision fully by expecting things to go well by managing and directing your thoughts.

## GETTING BEHIND YOUR DECISIONS WHEN THERE ARE NO ATTRACTIVE OPTIONS

Sometimes we find ourselves making decisions when it feels like there are no options that feel good. In these cases, it's best to find the option that feels better (or less bad) and then get into alignment behind that decision.

For example, for the first decade of our marriage, my wife and I did not have health insurance. We considered getting some every now and again. But once we started looking into plans, it simply felt better to us not to buy insurance.

Not having health insurance didn't *look better* (and certainly we didn't share this fact with anyone after getting some horrified reactions from some), but it *felt better* to us. And here's the thing about what feels better to you — it's not up for debate. Your feeling is completely personal, beyond the limits of logic, beyond what your family or friends think, and it's the *only* relevant fact to consider when deciding what's right for you.

We revisited this decision to not carry insurance when my wife became pregnant. An uneventful birth is not inexpensive in the United States, and certainly, without insurance, any complications held the very real potential of bankrupting us. I remember doing all the research and considering all the possibilities. Specifically, I asked myself this one question:

*Was I willing to lose our house if something unexpected happened with the baby rather than buy the insurance policy?*

Note that while neither potential outcome felt *good* to consider, one clearly felt "less bad."

Every time I went on the website to purchase a plan, I just could not click the BUY button. While I didn't want to go bankrupt from an unexpected event, the thought of trying to protect myself from such an unwanted event felt clearly worse. That's just what was true for us.

So we made the decision not to get health insurance. And no, even though this decision felt better, we were not 100% aligned with this decision.

In between making this decision and my wife giving birth, the doubts would appear. Doubts are not to be ignored, because we live in a vibrational universe that responds to how we feel. Simply put, sweeping things under the rug is a losing strategy.

Aware of this, when these doubts arose, cutting them off was my responsibility.

In some way, I would say, "I see you there, Doubt. I acknowledge you. But this whole experience is going to go really well for my wife and me."

Part of getting behind your wobbly decision is doing the work of allowing the thoughts you don't like. Did I want to lose our house to a medical bankruptcy? Of course not. Did I like this thought? Not at all. But I didn't *resist* that dark thought either. I let it appear in my mind and I didn't try to pretend it didn't exist. I allowed this thought until I reached a state of neutrality around it. In other words, by focusing on it for a minute or two, it shifted from being a *bad thought* to *just a thought*. Dropping your resistance to what you DON'T WANT is a key element to getting aligned behind your decisions.

Other times I'd imagine myself holding my healthy child or I'd just connect to the little mantra that "everything works out for me." Sometimes I might just listen to some music or take my dog for a walk — the point is that my wife and I would do whatever it took to get back into the state of feeling aligned with our decision. We spent enough time visualizing things going well for us that these aligned thoughts overtook our fears and doubts.

So, when you make a decision and then feel yourself getting wobbly, it's in your best interests to get behind your decision by doing the maintenance work of finding ways to stay in alignment with what you decided.

While my son had a lovely birth, he arrived with a case of jaundice. The doctor began ordering tests and wanted to keep him in the hospital for a day or two. Things could go very wrong from here, we were warned.

Before I could process things, I was alone in a cold room with a new nurse who jabbed my tiny son repeatedly in the foot to extract some blood for tests. In that moment, I'll never forget how helpless I felt hearing him scream and watching his pink body writhe in pain.

All of this felt very wrong to me. This was everything we DID NOT WANT from this experience. These were other people's decisions playing out before me, not mine or my wife's. Doctors. Lawyers. Administrators. It all had nothing to do with me and my family and what we had decided our reality would be.

We had expected everything to go so well, for everything to work out easily, and yet it felt like things had the potential to go off the rails of our desires quickly. Over the next few hours I called some doctor friends to get their opinions. I did some research. Really, I looked for (and then found) evidence to reassure myself, to find my courage, and to re-align with my decision — *my son was fine.*

Despite the protests and warnings from everyone in the hospital, we signed all the forms and took our baby home where he could be skin-to-skin with his mom instead of alone in a room under a heat lamp. We placed him in the sunlight (vitamin D helps eliminate jaundice) and in a couple days the issue was gone.

I feel a sense of pride retelling this story because getting behind our decision was not easy in this environment. For me, it was a vivid example of putting these words — these theoretical ideas — into real-world application.

Now the point of this story has nothing to do with health insurance. Or healthy babies. And it has absolutely nothing to do with the right way to have a child, because there isn't one. In no way, shape, or form I am advocating to anyone that you should follow this example, because it's just one way to manage feelings of fear and doubt. (Eventually, it felt better for us to get a health insurance plan.)

The point here is that when you make a decision— any decision — in order to stay in alignment, you need to have your decision's back.

This can be challenging and very often requires you to dig deep into your well of courage. Being awake and courageous is simply the price of being able to leverage your superpower of deciding and living in the magic.

# THE PRACTICE OF ALIGNING

PAY attention to the words that come from your mouth.

Remember you (and your thoughts) are the only thing in between you and having what you really want. More specifically, it's the habit of entertaining thoughts that run contrary to your desires that keep you apart from what you want to see.

Your thoughts are constantly and forever telling you how right you are. If there's something you've decided you really want and yet it never shows up, you know there's only one place worth looking if you want a different outcome — inward.

If you wish to understand how and when you move out of alignment with your desires, you'll want to begin to *watch your buts.*

Most any time you express your desire and follow it up with a "but ..." you are deciding to focus on thoughts that run contrary to your desire. And you're not going to have much success creating your desire when you fail to align yourself with the expectation of its manifestation. In short, if you don't fully believe it's coming, it most likely is not.

Again, this is a habit of thought, and very often our awareness of our habits is rather low and habits can be challenging to break. The superpower of deciding is available to you right now, but to leverage it, you're probably going to have to change your approach to life. The biggest challenge to this approach is a willingness to set the truth to the side and place your desire in the center.

Yesterday, I coached a woman named Lisa around some of her desires for her life.

A single mom, Lisa shared that she wanted to write a book and create a coaching business where she could help people, do work she loved, and that would provide enough income to support herself and her son.

However, while she had taken the first step and decided what she wanted, her desire had little chance to manifest in her reality, because she was not aligned with her vision.

After clearly expressing her desire, in the next breath she told the story of how an illness she was dealing with would most likely derail her. In fact, she made this point to me three times in less than ten minutes. "I want this ... but here's why I can't have it," was what I kept hearing. When I pointed this out to her, she was unaware of her habit of thought, though she easily understood how the act of telling this story undercut her desires.

When I asked her to imagine how it would feel to be in charge of her own schedule, work with cool clients, make an impact upon their lives, and get paid well, of course she replied that this would feel really good. Likewise, when I asked her how it felt to tell the story of the illness that she was inserting into the equation, she said it felt heavy and unwanted.

In order to leverage the superpower of deciding, our desires and our thoughts need to be in alignment. You can't tell the story of what you want while feeling bad about any part of the story and hope that your desire will show up.

The pre-work here is to decide to become awake enough to notice whether the thoughts you choose are a vibrational match (that is, they feel the same) as what you imagine it would feel like to have what you want.

So when it comes to deciding to have what you really want, pay attention to the words that come out of your mouth. When you argue for your limitations, you get to keep them.

Making the case for why you cannot have what you want is never in your best interests, but it's worth mentioning why we fall into this habit. We do so because we've been trained to put the truth on a pedestal above our desires.

In Lisa's case, everything she shared about her illness being a disruptive force in her life was *true*. But keep in mind that we were taught to speak the truth about our current unwanted realities long before we were taught that we are the creators of our realities through the words we speak.

So, if the words you're choosing to speak do not feel good to speak, that's your indicator that your focus is in a place unlikely to serve you well.

If you're looking for a specific subject to monitor how your thoughts and words align with your desire, you can start with your relationship with money.

## PAY ATTENTION TO HOW YOU SPEAK ABOUT YOUR MONEY

Every year I go on a ski vacation. When an old college friend sees my pictures and hears my stories, he asks if he can join next year's trip. I tell him how much I'd love to have him join us. However, every year when I contact him to put down the deposit — to decide — he repeats the same story:

"Oh man, I'd love to go, but I can't afford it right now. Next year!"

My friend would be surprised to learn that he has told me some version of this story for most of the past fifteen years now. He's never gone on a ski trip. He's just gotten older.

I never say "I can't afford it" because my desire is to always have enough money to do or have what I want. When you state that you can't afford something you want — *even when this appears to be absolutely true given the numbers linked to your bank account* — the universe of your thoughts does its job by proving you correct. Remember, you are always right in whatever you decide, so it's in your best interest to be vigilant as to what you are professing to be true.

We forget that the real truth is that we are the deciders of exactly how much money we allow into our life at any moment in time through the degree of our alignment with having money.

Certainly there are some things I desire that I do not currently have the money to buy. However, because the thoughts of *I can't have that thing* or *I can't do that thing* feel so constrictive and downright awful to me, they don't linger in my consciousness. As a result, there are very few things that I desire that feel out of reach. At any moment, I have enough money in my current experience to do or have the things and experiences I desire.

However, if you're in the habit of connecting to thoughts like *I can't afford it* or anything else that asserts you don't have enough money right now to fund your big dreams or pay your mundane bills, here are some alternative thoughts:

*Right now, it feels better to say no.* (This simple decision leaves money out of the equation and makes you the director instead of the victim.)

*Now is not the time for me to decide.*

*Yes. I'll buy that. I know the money is going to show up.*

Many times in my life, from my first ski vacation in the Rockies, to buying our house, to investing hefty sums into my business, I've taken what felt like a leap of faith. I'd commit myself to something I currently did not have the money to pay for, because it felt better for me to do so. And without fail, because I was in such alignment with those desires, and it felt so good to say YES to, the money to fund those desires has *always* shown up, often in unexpected ways. You've likely done this many times. When it happens, it feels like magic (and it is), but hopefully now you can see that there's nothing random about your magical creations.

## LIVE IN EXPECTANT ANTICIPATION

While the majority of your decisions manifest right away, one of the most powerful things you can do for yourself when they do not is to practice being in a state of expectant anticipation.

One of my current bigger desires has to do with a cabin I want to build on my property. It's not there yet. I don't have all the money to fully fund it yet.

Yet.

But it will be. I've decided this to be so and I'm in a place of expectant anticipation.

So what does this mean?

It means I can feel the place right now. I'm building it in my mind. I dream about it regularly. I visit websites and collect design ideas and put them in a folder. I've been talking to my builder friends who can help me put my ideas into physical form. I imagine how fun it will be to write my next book there, to have a sleepover with my kids, to hang out in front of the fire with friends, good beer, and some guitars. I can hear the silence of the place (it will be off the grid).

Almost every day I walk to the property, right to the exact spot I've decided to put the cabin, and I spend a minute or ten thinking about what is to come. I measure out dimensions in the earth. This deliberate practice allows this sense of anticipation to gather momentum and expand. It's delightful to think about the place that will be. There's no part of me wishing it were here this minute, because I know putting this place together is going to be an adventure that I don't want to miss.

Every Monday I take the aligned action of transferring a set amount of money into a bank account for this cabin. It feels good to click the buttons. Seeing the total grow connects me to a feeling of *expectant anticipation*. I bask in the full knowing that my desire is making its way to me in a manner that truly delights me. When I was a child, I felt this expectant anticipation on Christmas Eve. These days, I feel the tingle when I see a foot of powder in the forecast and imagine what an exhilarating day I'm going to have on the slopes. The same is true when I start counting down the days to gathering with my old friends for a camping trip.

Really, this is just a smart way to go through life. You have an imagination, put it to work. Leverage this powerful tool that's always in your back pocket, wanting you to play with it. Get in the habit of looking forward to something every day. Make no mistake here. Dreaming takes work. It requires conscious effort and time to focus your thoughts and feelings in ways that please you (especially if they are focused on things that don't please you).

When you take the time to dream and live in a state of expectant anticipation, your life will be filled with experiences and creations worthy of expectant anticipation. Guaranteed.

Decide what you want. Imagine how wonderful it will feel to be in your life. Bask for a bit. And then move on with your life.

## DROP YOUR JUSTIFICATIONS

When I'm coaching someone about a specific desire they have, I always ask them WHY they want it. Try it sometime, and you'll notice how uncomfortable we tend to be with having desires even though nothing could be a more natural aspect of being human than wanting something new. When it comes to desires, especially ones connected to money, a common tendency is to justify what we want through noble intentions and rationalizations in order to preemptively defend ourselves from being painted with the selfish brush.

I run a program where I teach other coaches to write books for their business that will help them charge a lot more money for their coaching services. My whole pitch is make more money in your business with a book, so if we're talking on the phone, I know that person has the desire to have more money.

However, in our initial conversations, when I ask them why they're interested in my help with writing a book, 95% of the time, after some uncomfortable silence, they reply with some version of "I just want to help more people and make the world a better place."

Sounds nice, right?

But really, it's a cleverly disguised justification. These women believe it's not polite for them to just want more money for themselves and their families. So rather than just stating what they want from a place of alignment, out of habit they begin with a rationalization for what they want by placing their own desires a few tiers below some story about the greater good. What they are really saying to themselves is, "If I make the world a better place, *then* maybe I deserve the money that I really want."

Certainly there's nothing wrong with wanting to make a positive impact on the world. In fact, most everyone I speak with operates with this intention baked into the cake. It feels very good to help and make an impact. That said, I usually have to drill through several rounds of questions before people are willing to lay their naked desire on the table. It's not until I ask if it's important to them to create more money that they allow this desire to be expressed. (And usually when I ask, it's received as if the answer should have been completely obvious all along — *of course I want more money, that's why I'm here* — even though they'd spent the past ten minutes talking about everything but their biggest desire.)

The point is that burying your desire underneath a veneer of justifications and rationalization mutes your signal to the Universe. When you're justifying, you're hoping and praying to be rewarded for doing the right thing. But again, when it comes to manifesting your desires, there's only what you want and decide to allow. Right and wrong do not exist; the Universe is not keeping score, rewarding virtue and punishing excessive desire. You get what you decide, period.

The ultra-rich don't spend a moment justifying their private jet or why they have billions. These people are not rich because they are smarter than you. Nor are they more worthy than you. They are certainly not more pious, righteous, or deserving than you. Nor is there any amount of work or effort they could expend to justify the money in their account (and if there were, ditch diggers would be kings).

These people just experience their desires because they want to. They're not the least bit hung up trying to rationalize something that's operating beyond the norms of fairness or politeness.

Your justifications are just your doubts masking themselves in a manner that makes them appear to be more polite. But because you're always right, if you doubt you can have something you want, the Universe will always show how right you are.

Don't overlook this point. Take a look at an unfulfilled desire you have. Notice that you really haven't DECIDED to have this thing in your life, simply because you want it for the sheer personal delight of experiencing it. Take notice of how your rationale for *why* you want it is pulling you out of alignment with the desire.

Align with what you really want by setting your desires free. Let them loose, untether them from justification, seriousness, guilt, and rationalization. Want what you want.


PART II - ALIGN - SUMMARY

My desire for The View could not have been more clear.

I wanted this thing to be mine. For years.

85

I'd taken that first step in the process of deciding, to allow myself feel my desire, to not shy away from what I wanted, and to declare what I would have.

However, within myself, I wasn't a match for my declaration. Did I want this property?

Very much so.

Was I in alignment with having it? In other words, did I 100% think, feel, and act as if it were mine?

No, I wasn't there yet.

In fact, we just covered one of the biggest factors slowing me down — justifying my desire.

Really, I wanted the View for a beautiful place to party. I wanted to show it off, to feel proud of myself having the nicest view in the area, and honestly, I suppose I wanted to feel people admire me in some way. One can pick at the purity of my reasons, but they be what they be. When I finally surrendered to them, they allowed me to stay aligned with my desire.

For many years I picked at the worthiness of my intentions like they were scabs. In my mind, I couldn't just want the property for fun or to puff up my ego. To my thinking, these were selfish, silly, unworthy reasons. Instead, I approached my desire with a seriousness loaded with logic and pragmatism.

Recall that initially the land came attached with a house. While I never wanted the house at all (maintaining one home is enough for me), I spent a lot of energy trying to justify my having the View through the house.

I tried to think of how I could buy the house and property and turn it into a retreat center for my business. (Despite the fact that I'd grown weary and wary of hosting live events a few years ago.) In my mind, I could host workshops and retreats, and do work to make the world a better place, clinging to an old belief that if I had enough noble, practical intentions — the kind that would justify my desire — the gods would be more willing to reward me. But of course, this is the polar opposite of how deciding really works.

The thinking went like this ...

"I can have the View *if* I figure out a way to deal with this other mess that I really don't want to deal with at all."

It makes no sense when you write it out like that, and wherever there's an *if* associated with your desires, there is a lie. But when it comes to deciding what you really want, we're conditioned to justify our desires to ourselves and to "them."

However, if you want to manifest in ways that feel magical, justification is never your friend.

Eventually (through some wonderful coaching), I became aware of my justification habit and through deliberate focus, practice and time, I let it go by consciously connecting to a higher percentage of thoughts that supported my desire than those that ran counter to my having it.

I made the decision to focus on what felt better to me in the moment. Any time I'd catch myself thinking about where all the necessary money would come from, I'd direct my focus on how the vista always lifted my spirits. Any time I'd take a friend to see The View, I stopped telling the story about how I'd been trying to solve this puzzle of making it mine. Any time I'd look at the house or extra acreage I DID NOT want, I'd shift my attention to the section of property I wanted.

I'd stand in the field, take in the sky and the mountains, and bask in a state of appreciation of the beauty before me. And I stopped worrying about losing the property in the future, but rather I focused on the fact that for the time being, *right now in this moment*, the property was *mine*.

With appreciation, there was nothing to do, nothing to figure out, and nothing missing. These subtle but powerful shifts allowed me to get myself in tune with my desire, like turning the knob of a guitar string until it matches the frequency of the note.

And things were starting to sound quite good.

# PART III
# ALLOW

# THE VIEW STORY PART III: ALLOW

WHEN I RETURNED *from my trip, I got back to the business of focusing my attention on The View.*

*I asked several people for advice, but really what I was doing was bouncing their ideas off myself to see where I really stood with things and what felt better to me. When you're following your dream, truly deciding to have exactly what you want, everyone else's opinion is irrelevant.*

*While I was hoping the price would be about $25,000, I began considering what felt better to me in that present moment. A number came to mind that felt better than $50K. However, that number was only a little more than half of the asking price and some uncomfortable thoughts popped into my head.*

What if the seller is offended at my low offer and tells me to piss off?

What if this is my one shot, I blow it, and I lose the place forever?

*I spent a couple days, looking these thoughts directly in the eye, imag-*

*ining how those unwanted outcomes would feel. Certainly I wouldn't like them, but I arrived at the place where I knew I could handle them if they came to be.*

*With a thrilling sense of expectant anticipation, I sent an e-mail offering $27,000.*

*Four days later, I received the counter offer of $37,500.*

*I'd knocked 25% off the price. I was first in line. All I had to do was agree and BINGO, my dream would be realized. I should feel great, I thought. And yet, what would seem like it should feel like a GREEN LIGHT, simply did not. When I imagined writing the check for the amount they were asking, I noticed that my energy took a noticeable dip.*

*I felt through what I really wanted and arrived at a clear number in my head: Not a penny more than $31,500.*

*Was I really willing to lose my dream, a legacy for my kids and myself for what would amount to a drop in the bucket, a measly $6,000?*

*To my surprise, I was.*

*As forcefully as my rational mind urged me to act now and take the deal even though I couldn't find an easy sense of alignment, I noticed what felt better (not good, but better), and that was to do absolutely nothing for the next four days. (Many times I went to my keyboard to accept the offer on the table, but I never was able to type out the words without feeling like I was swimming upstream.)*

*So, once again, I let the property go.*

*Thoughts I'd been resisting came out into the light.*

Maybe this was always too good to be true.

It's likely that someone else will buy this property at this price now and it will be gone forever.

I'll regret missing this opportunity for the rest of my life.

*When I let these thoughts be what they were, when I stopped resisting them, a sense of relief came over me. I certainly didn't want to lose The View. But if I did, I would be okay. My life was already full of beautiful, wonderful things.*

*The morning of the fifth day, I woke and went immediately to my computer. I wrote the agent with an offer of $31,500 with the message, "this is all the chips I have to play with," and clicked Send.*

*It just happened to be my 47th birthday.*

# WHAT DOES IT MEAN TO ALLOW?

OKAY, so you've Decided.

Bravo.

And you've been Aligning as necessary.

Well done, well done.

In fact, you do this so often and so automatically with the vast majority of your desires that they manifest almost instantly.

However, if there's something you really want, but you can't see it yet, and you find yourself wondering whether it will ever show up, it's time to look to the third element of the deciding process and evaluate the degree to which you are ALLOWING your desire.

Remember, you are the creator of your reality (all of it), and your desires come to you because you decided to have them and then you allowed them into your experience.

Likewise, if you don't see it, this means that you are not a match to having this desire right now.

You decided to rise out of bed.

You decided to have something to eat.

You decided to read this sentence ... and so on.

These appear to be mundane because you do them and your manifestations are simply expected. So they happen easily.

When you don't hold any resistance to your decisions, the gate of Allowing swings wide open and the so fruits of your decisions manifest almost instantly.

But when we turn to the handful of desires that you have that do not show up in the manner or timeframe that you'd prefer, focusing on this third step of the process — Allowing — is a really good idea.

First let's define what it means to ALLOW.

Allowing means that you let your current reality be what it is in the moment, that you *stop treating the absence of your desire as a problem that needs to be fixed.*

In short, the last puzzle piece of deciding requires you to stop resisting *what is*, especially when you don't particularly like some aspect of *what is*. Allowing is another way of saying that *you have dropped your resistance.*

For example, say you're not feeling great in your body and you'd like to lose some extra fat, feel stronger, and look better.

However, if every time you get out of the shower and see your naked body in the mirror, you curse yourself and judge your body to be wrong, vibrationally, you're throwing up a wall of resistance.

Focusing on what you don't want or what you don't like while simultaneously hoping to create something you do want will prove to be never-ending frustration. It's the antithesis of deciding.

Allowing means that you are willing to take the path of least resistance. Of course this probably sounds easy enough — after all, who's not willing to take the easy way, right? However, don't make the mistake of thinking that the path of least resistance is a passive route. Rather, when you're really paying attention to your own thoughts and truly allowing *what is* to be okay, you'll notice that deliberately directing your thoughts toward what feels better is indeed, work.

Going back to the example of your body in the mirror, while the truth may be that you don't like your body in the moment, the work to manifest your desire requires you to be okay with your body, now. No, you don't have to pretend to be in love with your body when you don't like it very much. The "lipstick-on-a-pig" approach will never work. But yes, you do have to decide to do the work of finding thoughts (any thoughts) that move you out of the state of resistance.

You may even have to sit down and make a list of thoughts that feel better when you think them. Maybe you like your hair. Or your ears. Or the cute mole on your left pinky toe. Focusing on what you like about yourself helps. But maybe your feeling about your body is so strong in the unwanted direction that you need to turn your attention someplace completely different. Try taking a nap, walking your dog, or listening to some music. The bottom line is that in order to allow, your job is to *find a way to feel better, now.*

When you're in the state of Allowing you will have found the balance of being okay with having your desires … and at the same time, you will connect to thoughts that allow you to be okay with that desire *not* being here, manifested in this present moment. These thoughts are not contradictory, but rather complementary, working together through the power of the Universe to bring you your desire through the absence of resistance.

# WHAT DOES ALLOWING FEEL LIKE?

THIS COULD NOT BE SIMPLER.

You know that you're allowing by how you feel.

Allowing feels good. More accurately, allowing feels *better* (your aligned decision may not always feel *good* in the moment, but it will always feel better than a decision that holds you in a state of resistance).

Resistance feels bad.

That's all there is to it.

So if you feel some shade of bad — worried, anxious, exhausted, etc. — it's your job to fire up your superpower of *deciding to feel better now* so you move into alignment and allow your desires.

Very often, the key that allows you to feel better now so you can unlock your desires requires you to do the thing that feels the most intense, the most counterintuitive, and the riskiest — and that's to LET GO. So let's talk more about what that really means in your life.

## ALLOWING REQUIRES YOU TO LET GO

The real key to allowing is to let go. Now, you've probably heard about the concept before, but in order to leverage the power of deciding, this idea of letting go needs to start showing up in your life in a practical manner.

Letting go and allowing means that you have dropped your resistance.

While that might seem simple enough, very often it's the part of the deciding and manifesting process that requires the most attention.

More specifically, when we're talking about dropping your resistance, what we're really talking about is giving up the struggle, the striving, and the pushing in favor of deliberately turning your attention to thoughts that allow you to feel better, now.

In short, your job here is to decide what you will have and then get out of the way.

## WHY DO WE STRUGGLE TO LET GO?

Letting go is putting the Universe of your decisions in charge and allowing the road of your life to rise up and meet you. You give up trying to *figure it out*, you let go of trying to *make it happen*, you set aside motivation and pushing to get it done. Instead, you remember that the Universe is following your lead, arranging itself in alignment with your decisions and desires, and you allow what you want to come to you, just because you want it.

You didn't come into this experience to be the maker — you came here to be the one who imagines and the one who delights in the process of creating new things. You came here to be the receiver of your desires. You didn't come here to sweat over the hot stove, you came to savor the pleasing flavors and textures of the meal in the lovely dining room. When you let go, you are letting the cooks do their job and staying out of the kitchen.

Even if these words resonate within you, the idea of letting go and allowing runs at odds with dominant cultural beliefs and norms. No one is teaching you to relax your way through life and to use the power of your thoughts and intuition to create your desires. On the face of it, letting go and allowing seems like a highly impractical approach to living. It's the antithesis of what you were taught in school, and most of us were told we needed to eat our mushy peas if we wanted dessert. Given how we have been taught to strive our way through life, to be vigilant in protecting ourselves from unwanted outcomes, it's not at all surprising that we struggle with letting go.

The message we've internalized is that if you stop making it happen, you're entering dangerous territory. However, you very likely already know that the make-it-happen approach feels exhausting.

Personally, I've never come across an over-achiever type whom I thought was truly relaxed and happy. They are driven by a relentless fear-of-failure anxiety. I remember being in graduate school, striving for my Ph.D., believing that if I suffered long enough doing things that I didn't like very much, someday, I'd be successful like the professors who were teaching me. One day it dawned on me that almost none of those professors seemed very happy.

While deliberately choosing a "let it go" approach to your desires may appear to be abnormal compared to the just-do-it approach, you're not reading a book about leveraging your superpower of deciding because you're looking for more normal experiences, are you? Let's dive into some practical ways to start letting go and allowing your desires.

## YOU ALREADY LET GO ALL THE TIME

You let go, or more specifically, drop your resistance to move yourself into an allowing state, all the time.

So even if you think you don't know how to let go, you're already an expert. In order to leverage your superpower of deciding, you just need to refocus your awareness and practice.

Letting go means dropping your resistance, by turning your attention away from thoughts of what you DO NOT want.

When you fall asleep each night, you let go and allow.

When you immerse yourself in something that pleases you, like music or perhaps a film or TV show, you let go and allow.

And if you meditate, it's not that there's something mystical about the breathing or any mantras. The benefit of meditation is that by focusing your awareness in a neutral place, you are suspending any thoughts that run contrary to your desire. You distract yourself, allowing your desires to flow in through the back door, the crack of least resistance.

For example, with The View, for most of the time I was focused on how I needed to buy all twenty-three acres and an extra house I did not want to meet my desire. Focusing on the form, in my mind there was no other way, and so there were many resistant thoughts within me.

When I shifted my focus on the essence of my desire — the feelings of expansiveness, freedom, beauty, and appreciation I felt from the View — the road rose to meet my desire.

When you decide to change your mind about something, you let go and allow. Maybe that flight delay is perfect, rather than a problem to dwell upon or try to solve.

When you focus your attention to how it feels to *have* what you want rather than what you have to *do* in order to get what you want, you let go and allow.

When I stopped thinking about all the gymnastics I'd have to do to create all the money I assumed I'd need for The View and started enjoying the land as if it were already mine, everything shifted in my favor.

You already know how to do this stuff. We're just talking about tweaking your focus by remembering to deliberately direct your thoughts in ways that benefit you.

# THE PRACTICE OF ALLOWING

## GIVE UP NOW

GIVING up now is one of the most powerful things that you can do. Really, it is. When you give up, you give up your resistance. And when you give up your resistance, you clear out the cobwebs that trap your desires. You stop trying to manage situations that are not intended for you to manage in the first place. You stop pushing and striving for your desires, because the pushing and striving feels worse.

We're reluctant to give up because we're taught to pursue our desires in the exact opposite manner. We live in a world of motivational slogans designed to show you how you need to hang in there, to work harder, faster, smarter, all so you can struggle your way to your dreams.

But deciding doesn't really work that way. If it did, there wouldn't be anything that felt magical about your superpower of deciding.

Your job in creating what you really want is to decide, align, and allow — to focus, to feel good, and to let go.

If you're doing something that doesn't feel good to you, stop doing it. This is what giving up really means in your day-to-day experiences. If it doesn't feel good to you, it's not meant for you. Period. That's how your intuition is working tirelessly on your behalf to guide you down the path of least resistance to your desires. When you take actions based on them *feeling better when you do them* rather than taking actions based on *what you think those actions will get you*, you are giving up. That's a good thing.

It doesn't matter what strategy worked for your friend or your mentor. It doesn't matter how good the idea looks on paper, or whether it makes logical sense. It doesn't matter what you were taught regarding the right way to do something. It doesn't even matter what worked for you in the past. If you are taking an action that does not feel good to you *now* based on a belief that doing it will get you something you want *later*, you've veered off the path of allowing. This will only delay your experience of getting what you want. Your job is to tune yourself into what feels better. Then have the courage to follow where that path leads.

When you're mentally or physically struggling, give up. You can't suffer your way through the story and expect it to have a happy ending. You already know that when you let go of something you've been battling with, you see the whoosh of how things rearrange themselves to your benefit. When you give up the struggle, you notice the immediate feeling of relief. Relief always feels better. Relief is your indicator that you've stepped out of the way of your own intentions and flung open the gates to allowing. Letting go means that instead of making it happen by force or through what you DO, you open yourself to the magic of allowing by pointing yourself in the direction of what feels better right now.

In order for your decisions to manifest, you need to be a willing component that easily allows yourself to have what you want. Very often, this requires you to get out of the way and let the Universe do its job of assembling the components and arranging the timing and details. Your job is to decide what you want, to align with having it, and then allow it to be served to you. Your job is not to run into the kitchen and to start coaching the chef how to best prepare your meal.

Giving up now is not complicated, because metaphysical ideas are always simple. You do it all the time when you take a nap, you play some music, you enjoy a meal — anything that distracts you from thoughts that don't align with your desire. Give up and give in to the well-being that surrounds you. Remember that everything you want is downstream. In fact, you can give up right in this moment by taking a deep breath and exhaling and resetting your awareness to something that pleases you.

Whenever you're feeling stuck, you can always just say, "Universe, sort all this out for me. If you need me to do something, tell me what to do." Through the years, I never acted on any of my ideas to own The View property because they all felt too complex, too complicated, and too far out of my reach. No actions felt easy, simple, or good, so doing nothing was the better-feeling choice. My desire remained strong, but I was simply too tired to fight for it any more. Without being aware of it, by giving up and letting go, I was unlocking the door to allowing the Universe to lead me directly to my desire.

When I met my new neighbor Rich, thinking he'd bought The View, I congratulated him on his beautiful new piece of land.

When he said he'd not bought the parcel I was referring to, I knew to call the realtor immediately. I didn't have to strategize or deliberate. Likewise, in time, I knew to call my lawyer and my banker. Once I let go of forcing the actions I thought were necessary (and never felt good), all of the truly necessary actions were obvious and easy. That's the power and clarity that emerge when you truly give up. And that's how you activate your hidden superpower of deciding.

## BE WILLING NOT TO HAVE YOUR DESIRE

"Huh?" you ask.

"This guy writes a whole book about my superpower to decide to have what I want, and then toward the end he tells me to be willing NOT to have it?"

Yes. I just did that.

Remember, your job is to decide.

Your job is to direct the universe of your thoughts toward your desire and choose thoughts that align with the having of your desires.

But sometimes it'll feel like you've decided and aligned — you know what you want, and you're vigilant in the thoughts that you choose about that desire. But, still, nothing shows up. And very often, the continued absence of your desire leads you to feel anxious, doubtful, or afraid.

In these moments, the most powerful thing you can do is to give up and surrender to the thoughts and feelings.

Specifically, imagine what it is that you want. And now imagine what it feels like to never have it.

Let the feelings come, whatever they are.

Shame. Disappointment. Fear. Resentment.

Let the thoughts flow through your mind, let the feelings wash through you. Allow yourself to be willing to think these thoughts and feel these feelings that you've been resisting because you thought them too overwhelming, shameful, or dangerous. (In the law of attraction community, a common misconception is that unwanted thoughts cannot be entertained for even a moment, because one's focus must be always be positive. However, trying to avoid thoughts you don't like breeds the resistance that keeps you locked in a holding pattern with your desire.)

When you stop resisting the feelings that you don't want to feel (i.e., *what if I never get what I really want?*), when you just sit with them for a few moments and allow them to be what they really are — energy that wants to move — they will evolve and the energetic logjam within you will break apart. Your desires are free to flow to you once again.

Going back to the example of The View, while I decided that I wanted this property the instant I saw it, I spent the intervening decade trying to figure out different schemes to *make it happen*. But none of these approaches felt close to being aligned and the energetic approach to *making something happen* is at odds with the energy of *allowing something to happen*.

Things would not change until I was truly willing NOT to have my desire.

One day several years ago, while walking our dog to The View, my wife Karin encountered a man named Steven inspecting the house attached to the land. He introduced himself and informed her that he'd decided to buy the home and property.

I let her words sink in. Little by little I'd been preparing myself for this day. I knew the property wouldn't stay on the market forever, and I'd exhausted every strategy I could conjure to acquire it.

I remember thinking to myself, "Okay, it's gone. Now what?"

Karin continued to share what she knew about the buyer. He was single, close to my age, and seemed like a nice guy. She thought we might be friends.

Hmmm, I thought. I'd like to have a cool new neighbor. I'd like to have a friend I could go sit on the porch with, enjoy the view and a beer. Local friends are few and far between in the rural area where we live. Maybe this will work out.

Looking back, it was in that moment that I dropped my resistance to NOT having this property that I wanted so badly. In other words, I gave up.

I still wanted it, of course. The intensity of my desire did not dim.

But I was okay with not having it.

To be clear, I wasn't happy about not having it. Not at all.

I was just okay.

Vibrationally, I dropped my resistance to NOT having The View.

Yes, I wanted it.

But I was willing NOT to have it.

In the moment of losing it, I gave up working for it, pushing for it, and trying to figure it all out. And looking back, underneath my feelings of resignation, there was sliver of relief. (When navigating through the step of allowing, always follow the feelings of relief.)

## SURRENDER TO THE THOUGHTS YOU DON'T LIKE

When it comes to desires that have not yet manifested, you're likely focusing your attention on thoughts about the subject that you don't like. The problem comes when you try to overcome these thoughts, when you treat them as a problem to be solved, or as things that you want to go away. In these cases, where you're resistant to the thoughts you have and that you don't especially like, you neuter your superpower of deciding and delay the experience of having what you really want.

As much as I wanted this beautiful piece of land to enjoy and share, much of my thinking revolved around a single, powerful unwanted thought — *I didn't want someone else to beat me to the punch.* I didn't want to lose out on this opportunity. In an attempt to hammer this unwanted thought into submission instead of deciding, aligning, and allowing, I tried every strategy I could think of to make a deal happen. But each of them ultimately went nowhere.

By imagining how it might be okay for someone else to own my dream, I surrendered to the thought I'd been fighting and resisting for so long — *I don't want someone else to own this land.*

In allowing this thought, I dropped my resistance to my desire. And when you drop your resistance, you free your desire, and you allow the Universe to work tirelessly on your behalf.

A few weeks later after giving up on the land I wanted, I learned that Steven's deal fell through.

## GIVE UP "THE HOW"

Let's be clear.

You're not in charge of HOW things come into your experience.

You never have been.

Never will be.

Because you don't know HOW.

Your scope of awareness is limited, a tiny sliver of the possibilities the Universe sees.

Your job is to inform your reality what you will have by allowing your desires to come to you through the path of least resistance.

They will when you let them. And you know this to be true.

But when it comes to our desires, quite often we tend to fixate on the HOW.

We take responsibility for over-managing and controlling the how (instead of allowing), to the point where it usually backfires. We focus on the HOW based on the illusion that we *control* our reality rather that *direct* it.

Your job is to direct your reality from Point A to Point B and then get out of the way. Again, this is something you do all the time, when you're deciding and allowing. For example, imagine you're flying from New York to Paris. You follow what feels better, like getting to the airport, buying some overpriced snacks, and then stepping on the plane. Six hours later you're eating croissants on another continent. If you stop and think about all the things that went well in order for that to happen, it's mind-blowing.

But we don't tend to give these miracles a second thought, because we are such master manifestors that such miracles take place all day, every day. The point here is you decided to go to Paris and so you got to Paris because vibrationally you decided that things were going to work out, and they did.

You didn't inspect the plane to ensure its flight worthiness. You weren't monitoring flight paths and weather conditions. You didn't head up to the cockpit and wrest control from the pilot. No, you sat back, had a drink, watched some TV, and tried to get some sleep.

The point here is that the majority of your life works this way. You decided how your reality would be, and so it is. It's easy to overlook that everything in your life is following your lead, because we tend to focus more on our desires that have not yet manifested.

But if something is unpleasing or not showing up on our timetable, we often fall back into our conditioning and try to control our reality instead of directing it. We stop enjoying the flight and relaxing and instead make our way to the cockpit to fiddle with the gauges and controls (even though we have no idea how to really operate them).

Notice the vibration of needing to control something. It's on the same frequency of the fear of something not going according to plan. Trying to manifest your desire from fear has a long and poor track record.

You've probably noticed that the people who try to control every aspect of their lives are the ones who are frequently disappointed and filled with anxiety. They are also not fun to be around. When their attempts to control how things work fail, they become more anxious, squeeze tighter, and there's a vicious cycle underway. The good news is that eventually they will exhaust themselves, perhaps through an illness, and give up and re-enter a state of allowing.

Compare this needing to control reality to the feeling of directing your reality with the presence and certainty of a queen or king. A queen simply commands what will be done and then proceeds with the knowing that her order will be fulfilled. Through your superpower of deciding, you always get to choose whether to control or direct your reality. In those moments, be like the queen.

And here's the real reason to let go of needing to control the HOW of your desires ...

You don't know the HOW.

You don't.

Think about something big you want.

Go ahead. Take a moment to find it.

Okay, now that you have this desire, ask yourself HOW you are going to manifest it.

Your answer to yourself, vibrationally if not literally, is "I don't know."

Because you do not.

And that fact is not a problem in any way because *how* your desire comes to you is none of your business.

The problem is that when you focus on feeling like you don't know, you are focused on your doubts. You pull yourself out of alignment with your decision. You fail to consistently have your decision's back. And this will make it much less likely to manifest, which in turn might lead you to attempt to control your reality through more plans.

Returning to the example of The View, what made the whole experience so delightful was that after letting go, I began to feel everything working out for me in specific ways that I never could have imagined. I was just along for the ride.

I am still astonished as to how everything was created for me in ways that felt so perfect, precisely because everything was unfolding beyond anything I could have orchestrated or planned. That's where the magic lives.

Remember, I had no idea that the property was divided into two separate plots of land. What's more, I never would have even discovered this unless my new neighbor inexplicably decided not to buy the most beautiful three acres, even though he had the money to do so.

And it just so happened that the exact boundaries of the three acres my new neighbor declined to buy constituted the exact dimensions of my desire. Everything I did not want — the house and surplus acreage — lay on the other plot of land. Finally, the asking price was now in the range of my reach. There was no longer a financial issue for me to try and figure out, but rather the question of what I would feel good paying for the property.

Again, my very selfish inspiration for writing this book is so that I remember that the real power, the fun, and the magic is in the willingness to allow and be a cooperative ally to my wonderful partner, the Universe, which is continually serving up a steady stream of my desires.

The perfection of how this story unfolded for me was a direct result of my giving up trying to control the how. When you step into this level of allowing, from the outside your life will start to appear to others as a fortunate stream of coincidences or lucky breaks.

But you'll live in the deep satisfaction of knowing it is neither.


## HAVE IT NOW

Let's get metaphysical again here for moment.

In order to manifest something, you must be a vibrational match to having it. Again, look up for a moment, look around with fresh eyes and see all the things you've successfully manifested in your life simply because you decided to have them and held little or no resistance to having them. It's astounding.

Conversely, for that tiny fraction of your desires that have not manifested yet or feel like they never will, you can be assured that you are not currently a vibrational match.

One of the fastest most efficient ways to allow your desire into your experience is to practice HAVING IT NOW.

Now, this requires you to take charge of your thoughts and guide them. Your job here is to tune yourself into the feeling of what having that specific desire manifested in your life feels like.

When you feel it now, you have it now. When you have it now, you enter the state of allowing.

Let me give you a personal example about money.

For as long as I can remember, I've always had more than enough money in my life. That doesn't mean I've always had a lot, but I've had *enough*.

So a common desire is for me to have at least $20,000 in one of my checking accounts.

Recently I hit a wave of expenses for about $12,000. After

paying those bills and seeing the number in that account drop, an old thought gets activated — "Will I have enough?"

(It's worth noting that in that moment, objectively I still have plenty of money to do anything I really want or need to do — I have other bank accounts, savings, investments — but my fearful thought leads me to worry about the possibility of an uncertain future.)

Now, worrying about whether or not I have enough does not feel good. At the same time, this contrast launches a clear desire within me — I want more money in my account. And why do I want that money? Because I believe it would make me feel better.

Here's the important point to consider in HAVING IT NOW. If an extra $10,000 came into my account right now, how would I feel?

Well, over the years I've had this experience many times. If I were to attach words to my inner thoughts, they would be something like this: "Oh yeah, cool! That's awesome. I look forward to telling Karin later." (Twenty second pause) "I wonder who's pitching for the Yankees tonight?"

So when it does happen, I don't jump up on the table and do a happy dance. I don't get on my knees thanking the heavens in disbelief. Instead, I feel a moment of sweetness, I feel the warm wave of relief of having allowed my desire, and then I move on.

My point is that the reason I want this desire is really because I want to feel free and relaxed (I just happen to associate money with these feelings).

So, in order to be in a state of allowing my desire for money, I must feel relaxed and free NOW. In order to manifest my desire,

I need to practice HAVING IT NOW by guiding myself to feel relaxed and free, now.

One specific place where I feel free and relaxed is in nature. The more I go on daily walks with my dog immersing myself in moments that feel good, the more my vibrational state becomes a match for having more money.

Another reason I want money is because I believe having money allows me the freedom to have fun. (Whether that's really true isn't relevant. The fact that I believe it is.)

One of the most fun things in my life is to take a mid-week day off, head to a local ski mountain, and bask in the glory of one of my favorite pastimes. My whole life feels free on these days and I feel like a truly wealthy man.

Over the years I've noticed an interesting pattern. I cannot tell you how many times after allowing myself a fun day on the slopes I've come home to unexpected money — and that's even more fun.

Like attracts like.

Making the decision to have fun NOW, creates more fun things.

Allowing your desires NOW allows more of your desires NOW.

(As an aside, if you're reading this thinking, "I'd like more money to show up unexpectedly in my life too, Drew. But I have a job with a consistent paycheck, not a business where new clients can just show up," notice that the thought, no matter how logical, does not feel good. It's your signal that you're in a place of resistance, cutting your desire off at the knees. Instead of dwelling here, it's your responsibility to decide, align, and allow.)

Whatever it is that you decide to have, when you're truly

deciding to have it, you get yourself in vibrational alignment with having it in your life now. You cannot wait until your desires manifests to feel better. This defies Universal Law that states that you are a vibrational match for everything that shows up in your life.

Because when you allow yourself to tune into the feeling of having your desire now — in this case freedom and relaxation — you'll notice that you DO have what you want (even if the money hasn't hit your bank account yet). When you feel the presence of your desire now and bask in those good feelings, you affirm that it's yours. When you *know* it's yours, the Universe responds in kind, without exception.

In this example, from the contrast of feeling as if you don't have enough, you give birth to the decision that you will have more money. By doing the work of HAVING IT NOW, you consciously align yourself with the having it. When you tune into the feeling of having it, you drop the static of resistance.

When it came to The View, along with giving up on the need to make it mine and dropping any thoughts about how to make it happen, I entered the practice of having it now. When I stopped approaching the land as a problem to be solved, I just went up there and appreciated the hell out of the place. I'd go for a ski or a walk. I'd imagine where I'd put my little writer's cabin and what the design would be like. I'd take in the sunrise, I'd watch the afternoon shadows creating the contrast that revealed new secrets about the topography of the hillsides, or I'd wait in anticipation for the full moon to rise over the mountain. If I was alone, I'd just bask in the wonder, the beauty, and the silence. And if I brought a friend or two, I felt as if I were sharing my view with them. Because I was. In those moments, The View was mine. I didn't have a deed in some drawer, but I was standing there, having it in all its glory, enjoying the hell out of myself. I didn't need to wait for a piece of paper to have what I wanted. I only had to allow myself to bask in what was right in front of me to have it now.

By allowing myself to have what I wanted *now*, there was no lack. There was no problem. Because I was now tuned into my desires, a full match for what I'd decided to have, the rest of the details just fell into place. And really, the rest is just details. Your work is the deciding, aligning, and allowing.

Handle that and the manifestation will follow. Always.

# THE VIEW STORY PART IV: THE MANIFESTATION

THREE HOURS *later Bob's number buzzed on my phone again. I was sweating from the August humidity and my heart hammered with anticipation as I answered the call.*

*"Well, Drew ... I presented your offer in your own words to the seller and she got back to me right away. They will accept your offer," he said.*

*My first thought was* I can't believe it!

*My second thought followed quickly after.*

I KNEW IT! I KNEW it!

---

THIRTY MINUTES *later I sat in Bob's kitchen a mile down the road from me, and wrote the deposit check.*

*I floated through the rest of my birthday, the best one I can remember.*

*Before I went to bed I went out on my deck and soaked in the starlight.*

*"I did it. I did it. I did it," I kept chanting to myself. I probably said this three dozen times, basking in the phrase. I raised a glass to the constellations in celebration.*

*All night, my body hummed like a tuning fork. I've never felt a sensation like it. I don't think I slept more than an hour or so, yet I was wide awake when the sun rose.*

## PART III - ALLOW - SUMMARY

When I closed on The View, I got exactly what I wanted (and nothing that I did not want) at 5% of the price that the home and twenty-three acres went on the market for originally.

Even though I've owned The View for over two years now, I remain as proud of this creation as any in my lifetime, likely because it represents the culmination of decades of study and practice of the art of conscious creation (or law of attraction, if you prefer). Through this experience of creating The View, I'd taken most every theoretical concept I'd learned over the years and put them to the test of real-world application.

I decided I wanted it the moment I saw it. I spent many years getting into alignment with that desire. And I learned to let it all go to the point where I allowed this desire in my life.

This stuff works.

If given the choice between being handed a winning lottery ticket for a million dollars or manifesting The View in the precise way I did, even though the unfolding lasted over a decade, it would not be a contest. For me, it is sacred ground, because it's a living, tangible, and very personal reminder of the power of deciding, aligning, and allowing.

The story of this land and its significance to me and my family is just beginning. I am already imagining what comes next in terms of what kind of structure I will build to host the gatherings that will follow. But more relevant, every day when I hike, ski, or drive up to visit this property, upon taking in the vista I'm uplifted by the thought, "Oh wow. I really did call this into my life, didn't I? It all really happened — just because I wanted it to happen."

In those moments, I'm reminded of the power within me to direct the course of my life, and that I do really possess a fantastic superpower. I need only remember to apply it in order to decide my way to my life's newest desires.

My hope is that through this story and these concepts, I have reminded you to do the same.

- Drew

P.S. If you'd like to see some photos of The View, visit www.verycoollifebooks.com/view.

# DID YOU LIKE THIS BOOK?

IF SO, please consider reading my other titles.

VISIT WWW.VERYCOOLLIFEBOOKS.COM for the complete bibliography and special offers.

## REVIEW THE BOOK

If you enjoyed this book enough to recommend it, please help me share my work with other like-minded people by leaving a review at the book's Amazon webpage. In the e-book version, you can also just scroll to the last page to be automatically directed.

Your reviews have a very powerful effect on book sales, so I thank you in advance.

## LET'S STAY CONNECTED

To learn of my upcoming books, free offers, coaching programs, and other very cool stuff, please join my mailing list by visiting www.verycoollifebooks.com

# YES, I WILL PERSONALLY COACH YOU

IF YOU RESONATED with this book, I'd love the opportunity to do what I do best — to personally coach you to integrate these ideas into your life.

To learn more about of my current personal coaching services and programs, please go to www.verycoollifebooks.com/coaching now and get in touch with me.

Please feel free to e-mail at drew@drewrozell.com.

I'd love to hear from you.

# HELPFUL PHRASES TO REMEMBER

EVERYTHING IS HAPPENING in perfect time.

Everything is paid for.

Everything works out for me, just because I want it to.

I. GIVE. UP.

Stop figuring out, and get into the flow of having.

I am in the exact right place, at the right time, with the right people.

Everything everywhere is helping me.

Everyone everywhere is helping me.

If I don't like it, it's not for me.

Things go really well for me.

My job is to get out of the way.

Gather evidence, notice all that you have allowed.

Simply take a deep breath. Relax. Let things be what they are.

I am always just ONE decision away from having what I want.

Printed in Great Britain
by Amazon